76 Ways To Get Organized For Christmas

and make it special, too

With illustrations by Susan Monson

Bonnie McCullough
and Bev Cooper

ST. MARTIN'S PAPERBACKS

Illustrations on pages 8, 19, 33, and 78 reprinted from *Homemaker's Executive Day-planner,* by permission. Illustrations on pages 25, 42, 62, and 76 from *Totally Organized.*

76 WAYS TO GET ORGANIZED FOR CHRISTMAS

Copyright © 1982 by Bonnie Runyan McCullough and Beverley Cooper.

All rights reserved. No part of this book may be used or reproduced in any manner whatsoever without written permission except in the case of brief quotations embodied in critical articles or reviews. For information, address St. Martin's Press, 175 Fifth Avenue, New York, N.Y. 10010.

Library of Congress Catalog Card Number: 82-5604

ISBN: 0-312-92940-4

Printed in the United States of America

St. Martin's Press trade paperback edition published 1982
St. Martin's Paperbacks edition/October 1988
Revised St. Martin's Paperbacks edition/November 1992

10 9 8 7 6 5 4 3

Contents

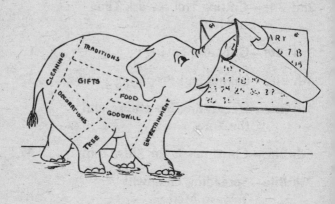

Introduction: There's More to Christmas Than the Tree and a Turkey!

This book is written for those of us who love Christmas, who love to make and buy and do, but who typically run out of time.

We enjoy the festivities—parties, reunions, concerts, and programs. We look forward to giving gifts to loved ones and seeing the special light that shines in their eyes as they open our gaily wrapped and bedecked offerings. We relish the traditions of preparing food and taking part in various activities centered around our families and our neighborhoods. We love the special and magical spirit that is all around us. We revel in the excitement and anticipation of getting together with those who mean the most to us at this special time of year.

As the season progresses, the gifts, the extra projects we have taken on, and the things we want to do begin to crowd our everyday life. Projects, parties, and programs intended for our pleasure and entertainment all become "obligations" and the fun is gone. If there is ever a time when we feel like we are living in a pressure cooker—this is the time! And to top it all off, other people tell us that there's nothing to getting ready for Christmas—just put up the tree and buy a turkey.

This book was written to help you carefully analyze your activities and traditions. Much of the pleasure of a happy Christmas is based on using good organizational techniques and time-management principles. These points are identified for you by numbers in the margin and by bold print. Keep a pencil or yellow marker with you as you read to mark ideas you want to use. We will help you create more time for your family and the projects you wish to undertake by making the optimal use of your available time. Then, because you can never do all the things you dream of, we will help you simplify and cut back to a manageable pace. If you are ready for more, we offer simple traditions to enhance the holiday, suggestions for the children, and meaningful ways to spread goodwill.

Put away the old cross-mess—being depressed, frantic, under pressure, and over budget. Have a Christmas in which you enjoy the ultimate spirit of goodwill, where there is peace and a relaxed atmosphere, and where you can enjoy friendships and kinships, without being left with a mountain of bills and unfinished projects. You can organize Christmas and make it a special time of year. Regardless of the temperature or the calendar date when you pick up and read this book, we wish you and yours a very Merry Christmas for the coming year and always.

—*Bev and Bonnie*

Start Now—You Can't Eat an Elephant in One Bite!

Preparing for Christmas can be an enormous job—like trying to eat an elephant. Obviously, it can't be done in one bite, and couldn't even if it *were* made of German chocolate cake! Elephant-sized tasks can only be eaten one bite at a time, and, likewise, **Christmas projects should be planned, divided, and prepared for**—one bite at a time.

Christmas projects and celebrations need some direction and boundaries if you don't want them to take over your whole life. Most of us don't have the luxury of devoting all our spare time during November and December to Christmas activities. All the things you want to do can bring pressure if you don't govern your wants into a manageable schedule. Conquering this can bring about an atmosphere of unity, drawing your family closer together. Christmas isn't sprung on us at the last minute. The date is always the same. We know there are 365 days between Christmases, and yet we find ourselves making annual statements like, "I can't believe it's nearly Christmastime again!" Let's face it, once Halloween is over, there are only seven weeks left and the pressure is on! As we mature through life, we tend to repeat behavior patterns. Some of us are addicted to a high level of pressure and find one reason or another to set ourselves up for Crisis Living. If you are threatening a burnout, put on the brakes by cutting back this season. You can change if you pay attention to the ways you overcommit yourself.

2 At this point you will need to **make some decisions as to your purpose in celebrating Christmas.** . . . Is it to draw the family together? . . . To impress others? . . . To have fun? . . . To increase spirituality? . . . Or just to survive the season? We not only want you to live through it, but we also want it to be *special.* Your priorities reflect these goals, and getting control of Christmas will help you reach them.

One year, on September 4th, a woman stopped at Bonnie's house to buy one of the first editions of this book. As she left, she paused and said, "I am certainly glad to get this book. It is too late for this year, but at least I'll have it for next. . . ." Someone, somewhere, started the rumor that the best way to get organized for Christmas is to begin in January. That only works for 5% of the dedicated Christmas lovers; the rest of us feel like failures. Here is the good news. Being organized doesn't mean starting early, it means understanding how much time and money you have to deal with; accepting it and staying within that boundary. You can be organized even if you don't do anything until December 10.

If you picked this book up on November 15th or later, the time for preplanning is past, but we will explain how to evaluate where you are in terms of money, time, and skill, and how to cut back to a reasonable load for your circumstances, and still have the fun of spontaneity, friendships, and giving.

Some people find Christmas shopping unbearable; they hate the rush and crowds. If you are one of these people, **you may be better off shopping**
3 **from a catalog or buying one gift per month throughout the year and stashing them.** Other

people love the impulsiveness of Christmas shopping and enjoy the sales promotions. Their best preplanning technique might be to **set up a Christmas savings account. It helps to collect some gift ideas throughout the year, even if you don't shop until the week before Christmas, and this exercise doesn't cost anything at all.** No matter when you begin to shop, or whether you delegate it to someone else, it will help to **make a list before you shop.**

A few people find it rewarding to begin planning in January, while it's still fresh in their mind. Obviously, making a few tentative decisions in January can put you ahead come November. By setting goals early in the year, you can **take advantage of sales and hidden moments of time.** For example, if you know that you want to make clothespin ornaments next year (because you saw some cute ones at the fair last year and bought a sample), you can buy the clothespins at the discount store when they are plentiful and only 97¢. If you know you want to give Aunt Sylvia's family an afghan for next Christmas, you can buy the yarn at the January sales and work on it each time you sit down to watch TV. But, remember, there is a difference between capturing spare moments and "working on Christmas all year long."

Yes, there's a lot more to Christmas than the tree and a turkey. Just like a huge elephant, Christmas can overwhelm us. What can you do to cope? Obviously, Christmas cannot be eliminated from your calendar or from your life, nor would you really want it to be. The answer is to divide this elephant into big chunks and then into bite-sized pieces. To help you pace yourself and see a clear picture of the whole season we suggest making several types of lists. Make an overall plan by setting interim goals and deadlines, all the while keeping up with your normal routine. You will want to cut the Christmas elephant into pieces by organizing housework, gift shopping, baking and food preparation, decorating, activities for kids, service projects, and memorable traditions.

After each Christmas, stop long enough to look back, evaluate, and make tentative plans for next year. As you use better management principles, you can have a successful season that builds friendships, nurtures compassionate service, brings peace and friendship, and lingers with warm memories. The pages that follow give ideas for each of the categories and tell how these chunks can be organized now . . . or be planned for throughout the year if you choose.

1st Bite—
Getting Organized

Let's get organized! To start, grab a piece of paper and pencil (not a pen) and a calendar. On the paper **write down all the things you want to do and need to do in order to be ready for December 25th this year.** You may still be adding to this list for several days as you collect data.

Recognizing early what needs to be done and then keeping on top of things makes the difference. Besides the baking, decorating, and gift giving, there are myriad little things that need to be taken care of so that Christmas can come and go leaving your sanity intact. The small details make the difference between Christmas and cross-mess! List in detail all necessary preparations for gifts, baking, cards, pictures, craft or sewing projects, decorating, etc. Some of these activities can be delegated, and the nice thing about preplanning is that when you are organized you are better able to utilize help from others, including spouse, children, and employees. Getting the list on paper is half the battle, and this particular list won't vary much from year to year, nor will the deadlines you set for the completion of most activities.

CHRISTMAS PREPARATIONS:		
ITEM	**TIME PERIOD**	**When Trans.**
Put up outdoor lights	Dec. 1-8	
Write family letter	Oct. 15-18	
Have family letter duplicated	Nov. 1-8	
Sew 2 sets placemats & napkins ~ gifts	Nov. 1-14	
Mail out-of-town parcels	Dec. 1	

Your list of preparations might include some of the following:

- Make out gift list.
- Shop for gifts to be mailed.
- Shop for gifts for friends and neighbors.
- Shop for gifts for family members.
- Sew placemats and napkins.
- Compose family letter.
- Have family letter duplicated.
- Take family picture.
- Write Christmas cards.
- Mail Christmas cards and letters.
- Wrap gifts for friends and neighbors.
- Purchase tree.
- Decorate tree.
- Put up outdoor lights.
- Purchase extra bulbs for outdoor and tree lights.
- Buy Christmas dresses.
- Clean house.
- Wrap gifts for family members.

Now begin to work with the calendar. Just like money, time in the future looks like it will cover a lot more than it actually will. Bring it down to reality. You will find it helpful to tape several calendar pages together so that you get a complete overview of the entire holiday season; six to ten weeks. (You will find these calendar strategies helpful when planning a big event such as a wedding or reunion.)

Pin down important functions by filling in the dates of activities and programs to which you are already committed. What day is school out? When will the company party be held? The church program? The school play? Piano recital? Craft sale? Dig deep into your memory of last year for parties, programs and obligations that may occur. Will there be a house guest? This may mean that housecleaning will take priority over other things.

Next, **put all the things to do and all the places to go on your calendar.**

9

1. Try to allow a time cushion for unexpected emergencies such as the dishwasher breaking down or the children getting sick. **Expect some unexpected happenings,** they always come.

10

2. Do not overschedule. In fact, try to underschedule.

3. If you have children, **reserve the last few days for the extra time the children will need with you and the little details you can't foresee.**

11

Use this planning strategy whether you start early in November or are down to the last minute. If you were selling tickets to a theater, you could let in only as many people as you had seats. Similarly, only so many extra projects will fit comfortably on your holiday calendar. Recognize when it is full and then stop. Writing plans on the calendar will bring them into a concrete visual dimension. If you are working a full-time job, have a new baby, care for an invalid parent, or have been ill yourself, take these limitations into account.

This exercise is not hard but it is vital. It gives you a realistic picture of how much you can take on without spoiling the pleasure of the holidays. Do not skip this written planning step. **Keep your plans in a specified place, preferably a planning notebook.**

12

At this point, if you are realistic, you may find that you can't do all the things on your list, so set priorities. **Decide what has to be taken care of and which things can be postponed or skipped,** using the basic "selected neglect" system. Look at each item on your calendar in terms of priority. Is this item something that NEEDS to be done or it just something you WANT to be able to complete?

13

Set up intermediate goals or deadlines for your projects on the calendar. When do you want to have those packages sent? By what date do you plan to have the cookies baked? Will you have a family picture taken? When? By what date do you plan to have cards and letters mailed? And what is the target date for being finished with the shopping? No two of us are the same. One couple does all the shopping the last two days before Christmas because there are so many good bargains—but they don't try to find a particular electronic game either! Gerrolyn, a wise, organized woman and mother of five, confided, "I try to have all my mother-only craft and sewing projects finished before December 10th. If they aren't, I simply put them away so I can ride the tide."

14

When you first work with the calendar, it seems there should be plenty of time for everything. It is so spacious. Stop to consider that in the United States the third week of November becomes filled with all the details of preparing Thanksgiving dinner and with children out of school. Don't count on the week before Christmas, either, for the last minute little things tend to swallow up your hours. The children's wants and involvements take up more time during this season with rehearsals, costumes, programs, or little gifts to be made for their teachers. More activity means more mess, which means more housecleaning. All these things multiply and complicate the season.

Break down your preparations as far as necessary. For example, if you chose the time period November 1st-14th to complete sewing placemats and napkins for gift giving, you could mark one day during that time period to "cut out placemats and napkins." On another day you would schedule yourself to "sew bias trim on placemats," and on another day to "hem napkins," so that the project will be completed during the period you selected.

Schedule a couple of different time blocks to write Christmas cards and address, seal, and stamp them. Enlist the help of young children to do the sealing and stamping, and the help of older teenagers to do the addressing. If you have cards and letters going to various points of the globe, write the date the card or letter is to be mailed in the corner of the envelope that will later be covered by the stamp. In this way, you can mail the cards as the deadlines come up, sending the overseas envelopes ahead of the local ones. Keep a simple address file by alphabetizing recipe cards in a 3" × 5" box. Put one family name and address on each card. There is room on the card for address changes and notes on dates of correspondence.

Keep this calendar and reassess it often. Continue checking your attitude to make sure it stays positive in spite of the normal tension and interruptions. If you sense you are feeling too pressured, evaluate your plans and see where you could elimi-

SAMPLE PLANNING CALENDAR

		2	3	4	5	6
31 Halloween	Nov. 1	2 Cut out placemats	3 Music lessons	4 Deadline—Duplicate family letter	5 Sew bias trim	6 Craft sale
7	8	9 Meeting	10 Sew napkins / Music lessons	11 Shopping	12 Deadline—Complete napkins and placemats	13
14	15	16 Shopping	17 Music lessons	18	19	20 Deadline—Bake fruitcake
21	22	23	24 Bake pies / Music lessons	25 Thanksgiving (no school)	26 Bake gingerbread for houses	27 Extended family party
28	29 Deadline—Mail packages	30	Dec. 1 Music Lessons	2 Deadline—Address cards	3	4 Host buffet for teens before dance

Tape several calendar pages together for a complete overview for the entire holiday season. Mark parties and programs; then fill in things to do and pace your activities into available time.

5	6	7	8 (half-day of school)	9	10	11
	School Craft Sale Deliver crafts 8:00 AM	Shopping	Music lessons	Band concert	Deadline—Adult-only crafts and sewing completed	Clean house
12	**13**	**14**	**15**	**16**	**17**	**18**
Deadline—Decorations up	Decorate gingerbread houses	School program	Youth carolling Music lessons	Deadline—Main gift shopping finished	School class parties Office party	Church social
19	**20**	**21**	**22**	**23**	**24**	**25**
Recital	No school	Clean house	Grandma arrives		Family night	Christmas Day
26	**27**	**28**	**29**	**30**	**31**	**Jan. 1**
Boxing Day Write thank-you notes	Kids' break-up-gingerbread-house-party (one friend each)	Clean house	Sledding party		Host New Year's Eve party	Take down tree and decorations

nate or combine some of the activities. Ask yourself: Is the world going to end if I don't do everything I hoped to do today? If the answer is no, then eliminate some of the obligations. To help you quit fretting about the things you are postponing until "after Christmas," write them on a Post-It Note and put in with your January calendar.

One of the main things to remember is that Christmas is about people, and you have to decide who are the most important ones in your life. They're the ones you want to spend your time on and with. You might have to eliminate some of the extras that would be nice to do but aren't really that important, in order to fulfill your goals of making Christmastime important to those closest to you.

2nd Bite—Cutting Housework Time in Half

While you are working on this Christmas elephant, don't let everything else go to pot. **Keep up on the basic household routine**—cooking, laundry, and pick-up—and you will have more time for Christmas projects and fun. **17**

Make the dinner decision before ten o'clock each morning. Better yet, during this busy season, plan the menu for a week and post it on the refrigerator door so other family members can get started on dinner preparation if you should be delayed. The longer you wait each day to decide what to cook, the fewer the choices. This one planning technique can make your day go much more smoothly. Men and women who are caught at five-thirty wondering, "What shall we eat?" often end up going out to eat, not because they want to eat out, but because they aren't organized. Without thinking, they may be using money they would really rather spend on something else. It isn't the cooking that is so difficult (you can bake chicken breasts in twenty minutes); it is the selection that is hard. Making the mealtime decisions early can prevent tension and save money.

Take some time every day to **maintain normalcy with a five-minute pick-up in every room** (a little longer in the kitchen). A tidy atmosphere builds self- **18** esteem and allows you the freedom to move on to other things. Start the pick-up at the front door where visitors can see. People don't notice the dust or smudges on the windowsills when they walk into a room; they notice the clutter. It is clutter that gives the illusion of a room's being dirty or messy. If you or your family or a visitor walks into your home and sees the living room neat, the assumption is, "This is a clean house." Then when you walk around the corner and see the kitchen messy, the conclusion is, "This is only a temporary situation." We are greatly affected by first impressions. If the entry is cluttered, we think that things are always cluttered in that house. Why not make this psychological principle work in your favor?

As you work, pick up the largest items first: cushions, newspapers, and magazines. Taking care of the biggest items shows immediate improvement, which is rewarding to the housekeeper. Spend just five minutes in each room, working as quickly as possible making beds, closing drawers and doors, wiping off, putting away, and straightening up. Don't put off picking up a room because "it needs a thorough cleaning." A pick-up will at least improve the room and keep it from getting worse. Stay on top of the clutter by taking time to straighten as you complete or interrupt a project. Allow your children interim pick-up times before lunch, dinner, and bed. Stop the mess before it becomes a monster. One homemaker takes care of her daily pick-up by putting away five things every time she walks into a room. By dinner hour, she has her maintenance finished. (She doesn't have young children who mess things up faster than she is working.) Concentrate on keeping up with the clutter; you can take care of the deep cleaning later. You can put a house on hold for several months if need be by daily allowing for pick-up, keeping up with meals and dishes, and tossing in a batch of laundry. Remember, keeping up is easier than catching up.

Falling behind with the laundry and dirty dishes will immobilize a household very quickly, leading to frustration, discouragement, and depression that blocks those Christmas plans. In one home, all the clothes are washed, pressed, and put away on Tuesday. It takes concentrated effort, but the clothing is out of sight and ready to wear six days a week. Another family has a system of washing one batch of clothes each day. Shelves were set up onto which the clean laundry is stacked, and everyone knows where to go if they run out. The shirts and blouses that need pressing are washed on Saturday when they can be immediately ironed. **Keep up with the laundry during this busy season.**

The most rewarding method for handling dirty dishes is to **take care of the dishes as they happen—** either rinsing them and stashing them in the dishwasher or washing them and draining them dry. The first thing to do when you walk into the kitchen to start a meal is to fill the sink with hot soapy water. Before starting to wash, put away any clean dishes from the dishwasher or drainer. Wash the utensils as they are used, making for faster clean-up later. It takes one-fourth the time to wash dishes that are fresh as to clean those on which the food has hardened. You would rather be doing something other than washing dishes, right?

To make more time for Christmas projects, learn the basic principles of setting priorities. Decide what has to be taken care of and which things can be postponed or skipped. Some people call this a system of "selected neglect." Here again, it often helps to write down your thoughts so you can evaluate them logically, using your physical senses rather than running ideas around and around in your mind trying to organize them. Analyze each item on your To Do list in terms of its priority—is this item something that has to be done, that needs to be done, or that you just hope to be able to complete?

The Christmas season is supposed to be the happiest time of year, but if it isn't, for those who are depressed it will help to: 1) stay busy; 2) avoid drinking and cut down on salt, sugar, and caffeine; 3) avoid overspending in an attempt to compensate for unhappy feelings; and 4) keep your expectations in line with reality. People and their faults don't change just for Christmas. Some people get despondent at this time of year because problems are magnified or because they worry about not having enough money, about having too many things to do, about encountering relationship problems, or about realizing how lonely they are. It will help to identify the source of the problem, because solutions vary with the cause. Naturally, planning and organizing will help with money and time shortages. Loneliness can be lessened by getting involved in a service project with others. If things are too stressful, avoid taking on any more; in fact, most of Christmas could be eliminated if need be. **Recognize that you can't do everything,** but if you start getting organized, you can get more done than you otherwise could.

21

3rd Bite—
Gifts and Giving

One of the biggest chunks of the Christmas elephant is gifts. Gifts are often a financial elephant as well as a time-consuming elephant; however, you'll never conquer this job unless you take the first bite, and that is to **make a list of everyone to whom you give gifts.** Use a chart, somewhat like the following, taken from Bev Cooper and Gayle Crook's *Homemaker's Executive Day-planner.* As you list the people on your gift list, leave space to **record several gift ideas for each person and indicate the amount you have planned to spend** for that person as well. At this point, add up the cost. If it's too much, go back and rebudget. It is better to do the shaving now than to agonize later over spending too much.

CHRISTMAS GIFTS:

NAME	GIFT	AMOUNT		Bought Made	Wrap'd	Mailed Given
		Budgeted	Spent			
Dean (Dec. 10)	robe	30 —	27 —	✓	✓	
	slippers	20 —	25 —	✓		
	peanut brittle	3 —				
John C	tie (Nov. 15)	8 —	7 95	✓	✓✓	✓
Nosgawa family	Gingerbread house (Dec. 20)	5 —	3 —			

As gift ideas are listed, if you have time and want to economize, think of things you could bake or make for each person. You can usually figure that a home-made gift is worth double the cost of the materials to make it if it were purchased at a retail outlet. Home-made or home-baked gifts are truly gifts from the heart and usually cost less. They are the most special of all and usually the most appreciated, but they do take time. If time is pressuring you, don't get an ulcer because you can't make all the gifts you would like to make. **Face your limitations. Cut down the list until it is within the time and budget you have available.** After all, aren't many of your treasured Christmas stories taken from the Depression days when families accepted their economic state and still found happiness? Peace, joy, and pleasantness don't necessarily come from having *more!*

24

Once the gift list is made out and the budget set, **give yourself a deadline by which to purchase or complete your gift selections.** Some organizers begin this list in January when ideas are fresh in their minds from last Christmas. They watch for bargains and use small moments of extra time. As the Christmas season gets closer, update and define your list more thoroughly.

25

If you choose, **as you bring the gifts home, wrap them** in Christmas paper, add a ribbon and tag, and tuck them away in a closet or on a shelf. Put a check mark in the "Wrapped" column and indicate where you stashed the gift so you won't forget about it. If the gift is to be mailed, wrap it in brown paper and strapping tape and put on the address label. It is also a good idea to write the mailing date in the top right-hand corner of the wrapped parcel (in a spot where the postage stamps will cover the writing).

26

If there are family members who might snoop at your gift list, devise a coding system to foil their plans. One mother just puts a 1, 2, and so forth in the "Gift" column and then has a master list of what those numbers mean, which she hides from her family. It is a little more complicated, but it works and discourages the snoopers in her family.

27

Keep Idea Lists

Sometimes making the gift decision is the hardest part of shopping. *What* would they like? **Keep idea lists for each family member including yourself,** simplifying gift giving all year 'round. This involves three phases: 1) asking for ideas from each person; 2) watching for clues and hints; and 3) keeping a written list of these items for recall whenever the occasion arises for buying or giving.

28

Even if you don't do anything else to prepare for Christmas from January to November, collect gift ideas. Gather ideas from hints others happen to drop and insights that pop into your mind all year long. Keep a page for each member of your immediate family with sizes and personal notes in your calendar/planning notebook.

Also, ask each person (mom, dad, kids, grandma and grandpa) for a "idea list", giving a peek into their feelings and desires. It may take several tries to get adults to talk about their wishes, but keep after them. Ask them to include **little inexpensive suggestions on the want list as well as dream items.** Have them be specific with titles for books, games, videos or music. One woman said she found the perfect motivator for getting her extended family to respond to her requests for gift ideas: "If you don't

29

send me your list by November 10th, I'll send your kids a kitten." If managed properly, asking for suggestions and keeping track of ideas can give you a glimpse of other's needs and wants. Knowing what will delight the receivers, lighten their work, or enrich their lives is rewarding to the giver. Keeping an idea list is handy whenever the occasion arises throughout the year and offers a starting point for Christmas giving.

To get a list from the kids, in the McCullough home, the children would start their lists from the Wards or Sears catalog. At first, they wanted everything. The young ones cut out the pictures; the older children wrote the words. (It was a good tactic to keep the kids busy while trying to fix dinner one night.) As the days went by, the children began to narrow their lists down to the things they really wanted most, and they rewrote the lists and posted them on the refrigerator. As parents, we did not feel obligated to give them what they asked for, but we considered their ideas. We tried to watch for a gift that would do something for the child to aid creativity, improve skills or serve some sort of purpose. **If**

30 **a child has his or her heart set on something you cannot or do not want to give, take time to let the child down gently and guide his or her wants into other territories.**

31 The art of giving is to **understand the people on your list and how they feel about things.** Do they treasure handmade items and the effort that goes into them? Do they like practical, useful gifts, or frivolities? Do they have a collection of cacti, antiques, porcelain dolls, clothes, or miniature trains? It is a challenging game to watch your friends and family for hints of gifts they will appreciate—and when it works, you both win.

Start an idea list for yourself. When the desire for 32
something comes, write it down. The Christmas
season may accentuate your own personal desires
and this will help you control them. When you get a
little money of your own, you can then logically
choose from your list the item you really want and
purchase it for yourself.

Keep in mind that every gift carries an obligation.
There are times when it is not fair to give, especially
extravagantly, because the receiver cannot handle
the obligation that goes with the gift—not just the
feeling that a gift must be given in return, but the
feeling of commitment that is due the giver. **Be sen-** 33
sitive to others and try not to make them feel un-
easy, obligated, or guilty by your generosity.
Keep those token gifts in line. A small gift of food
does not usually carry the same amount of obligation as some other things.

Every year in her national newspaper column,
Ann Landers prints a letter that goes about like this:
"Dear Ann: My husband has not worked for over a
year and we are just barely making ends meet. Is
there a tactful way to stop exchanging Christmas
presents? We can't afford to send any, and we don't
want any gifts, so how can this be handled?" Her
reply usually reads: "As I've suggested before,
around Thanksgiving, send cards to those on your
Christmas gift list saying, 'We are thankful for folks
with whom we can be frank. We are not in a position to send Christmas gifts this year, and we don't
expect gifts, but please accept our love and sincere
good wishes for a healthy, happy, blessed holiday.'"

Now I ask you, if you received a letter like the
one above from your sister asking to be relieved of a
burden of exchanging gifts, what is your inclination?
Since she is having a hard time, you would probably

want to help; more than ever you want to be generous. But if you send something, how would she feel? Guilty. Help her maintain her dignity. If you choose to send something, food carries less obligation than other tangible items. Perhaps you can wait and send something later, maybe you can send money anonymously through her minister. Only you can decide. Be sensitive to how your generosity affects others.

Keep Lists of Gifts Given

Keep your Christmas gift list. It will help you evaluate wisely the next time an occasion comes for gifts like birthdays, Mother's Day, Father's Day, and so on. These other-occasion gifts can be added to the Christmas record if you wish. You may decide to follow a theme or sequence of gifts, or you may choose to give unrelated items, but keeping a written record of gifts given will help eliminate duplication.

34 As long as you are getting organized, why not **keep a list of gifts you and your family received** and check them off when Thank-yous are taken care of.

Our feelings of goodwill and generosity blossom at Christmastime. This is wonderful, but our feelings often exceed our time and money. Look for possible solutions that you can live with. When you buy, try to pay cash or check. The cost of credit is no longer a minor item, it can add 5 to 21 percent to the purchase price. Don't let the twelve days of Christmas turn into the twelve months of payments. Green and red are the perfect colors for Christmas: People spend too much of the green stuff and wind up in the red. Keep control of your buying. It is possible to enjoy the fun of spontaneity and impulsiveness within a budget. (If you want the gift to be extra special, write a little poem or wrap it in an elegant style.)

Following are methods other men and women have found successful for keeping their gift giving under control. Don't forget, keeping a written gift list and evaluating it before you ever step into a store is the major source of control.

1. **To cut back on the number of gifts given each year, draw names.** Individual or family names can be drawn for your immediate family (your own household) or extended family (cousins, adult brothers and sisters). Names can be drawn

35

annually or set up on a rotating list that indicates several years in advance which person you will be giving to.

36 2. **Go together with others on some gifts.**

37 3. **Eliminate some gifts altogether.** The other person may feel the same way. They enjoy your friendship, but they would appreciate being relieved of the gift-exchange.

38 4. **Some gifts should be kept in the *token* category.** Offer a gesture of friendship—such as a loaf of bread or candy nibbles—but keep it small enough so that the receiver does not feel obligated to reciprocate.

5. Get over the idea that the size, expense, or novelty of a gift represents the depth of your love. **39** **Set an amount that is within reason for your budget, and then shop within that amount.** You can still be impulsive and have fun shopping, but you won't suffer the long, dry, out-of-money spell after Christmas. Sometimes it is the people who should spend the least who spend the most for Christmas gifts.

6. A friend in Arizona found her gift giving mushroomed because the items she had made and bought earlier in the year no longer seemed like enough when the Christmas season approached. The fun and excitement, the impulsiveness she felt at the time of purchase, had waned. She found it was better for her to save part of the shopping for December. Also, keeping a list of things she had already purchased, helped her not to forget about the things she had stashed away.

7. Bev Cooper, who works full time but still enjoys making things, said that she organized her gift giving by making her token friendship gifts throughout the year—usually ceramic ornaments. She likes to hand-make each of her children something, too, and this also is decided early and worked on during slack months. But she waits until a few weeks before Christmas to buy each child's main gift, to be sure that what she is buying is still what they want and that they haven't already bought it for themselves.

8. Another woman stated, "We all love hand-crafted items in our family, but I don't have time to make everything every year. Sometimes I buy beautiful things at bazaars and craft sales, almost for the cost of materials, and this money goes to worthy causes." Sales sponsored by organizations and auxiliaries, where the items are donated by the creator and then sold by the auxiliary, usually offer lower prices than sales where the artists sell their own work, because they have to calculate wages into their prices.

9. Jean's problem was that the earlier she started, the more she bought, and it kept escalating. The solution was to open a Christmas savings account, put in a little every month, and force herself not to start shopping until after Halloween. Giving the season a boundary helped her to cut back on regrets, mistakes and overspending.

10. **Watch out for time traps.** One busy mother, who also had a full time job, walked out of a December craft class thrilled about the white-felt tree ornament she was making, convinced that her four-year-old son would love it as a gift. The five-inch horse was to be hand-stitched,

40

stuffed, and trimmed with gold braid, sequins, and tiny beads, probably requiring five hours of work. Should she devote her limited time in December to something as insignificant as a tree ornament? How much is the child really going to get from this horse anyway? Do you think the mother will allow him to play with it? Perhaps it would have been better for her to determine to use the cute idea as a take-along project to work on during spare moments, such as coffee breaks during the next year, if, indeed, it was something she really wanted to spend her time on. This is where reviewing your priorities can keep you from getting sidetracked and over-committed.

As a thank-you token, the wife of a junior hight school principal decided to order and put on a special buffet of breads, cheeses, and cold cuts for her husband's faculty. The affair went very well. (The cost—over a hundred dollars.) Next year, the hint comes to do it again. Is she committed for life? Traditions start so innocently, but they can turn into bonds of slavery if you don't manage them.

Shopping Tips

Whether you are the type who enjoys shopping or someone who abhors it, try to put yourself in a better frame of mind. As you shop, think of the person you are giving the gift to and recall some of the special qualities in that person that you love and admire. This simple exercise will help to keep the special gift-giving spirit, make the task more pleasant, and avoid irritations from crowds or commercialism.

Following are some tips to use during your shopping trips:

- **Be kind to yourself. Don't worry about how glamorous you look while shopping; be comfortable.** Wear walking shoes, a sweater, and a light coat. You can always take the coat or sweater off so it doesn't weigh a ton on your tired shoulders. **41**

- **Take breaks during your shopping excursion if it is an all-day trip.** Have a glass of juice after about an hour and a half, then stop for a fun lunch break at an interesting restaurant, carry on for about another hour and a half, and then have another drink to quench your thirst before heading home again. **42**

- **Have your parcels wrapped and/or delivered if the store provides this service.** **43**

- **If possible, don't carry all your parcels around all day.** Periodically go back to your car and place them in your locked trunk for safekeeping and to lighten your load. However, it is not recommended that you leave packages where they can be easily seen as in a station wagon or hatchback. **44**

- **Streamline your purse and pockets** so they don't weigh 15 pounds, leaving only the essentials such as keys, wallet, checkbook, credit cards, comb, and lipstick, as well as your gift list. If you carry a purse, tuck it snugly under your arm to lessen the chance of having it stolen. **45**

46 • **Pay for your purchases by check where possible.** Carrying a lot of cash is risky and credit purchases tempt us to overspend.

47 • **Watch the newspaper for bargains** in all the major department stores—especially for items that are on your list. Special sale days are good for shopping but stores are often crowded. We suggest that you use these days to make extra-short trips just to buy those items on sale that you *really* need.

48 • **Preplan your trip by writing down the stores you wish to visit and map an orderly shopping route** to save backtracking. Follow this same principle in the larger department stores—don't shop on the main floor, the second floor, the main floor again, and then the third floor. Plan ahead to know exactly what departments you want to visit.

49 • Though it might be fun to shop with a friend, it is advisable to **go alone on the serious shopping trips.** A lot of precious time is lost waiting for your friend or visiting stores that aren't on your list. This same principle applies to your children —it is much kinder to leave them at home.

50 • **Save all sales slips and price tags.** Write the name of the item and the person to whom it was given on the back of your receipt in case you need to return any merchandise. Also, keep warranties and laundering or other instructions, and be sure that the tag indicates which items these relate to.

51 • **Beware of questionable shop-by-mail temptations and never send cash through the mail.** Be cautious about fraudulent charity collections, which abound at this time of year.

- **Try to shop at reputable retail outlets if there is a chance that the item purchased might need to be returned.** 52 Inquire about the store's returns policy and determine for yourself whether the item is worth the risk that you cannot return it in case of malfunction or other problems.

- Read warranties before you buy. This saves frustration later in case of faulty merchandise.

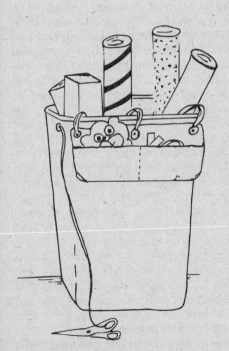

Create your own portable gift wrap center from a large wastebasket and utility apron.

4th Bite—Baking and Preparing Food

If your Christmas elephant includes making food, you will want to plan and organize this activity. In your mind, review last Christmas's baking. Did you do too much or too little? If you had shortbread cookies that didn't get eaten until March, then this year don't bake as many. On the other hand, did you run short of goodies last year? Did you gain 10 pounds because there were too many? Ask your family what food items they *really* enjoy most at Christmas. From the answers you get, plan this year's baking, eliminating the items that weren't favorites unless they are something that you really like yourself. Sometimes we grow up thinking we have to make certain traditional foods, no matter what. Evaluate. Maybe your family has never enjoyed these as much as you thought they did. Some folks like dark fruitcake and some prefer light fruitcake, while others don't like either. If your family likes a bit of both, then have a friend bake the dark and you bake the light, and trade. You might find that your Christmas baking is much simpler this year and that your family members really enjoy items that aren't so rich, heavy, and calorie-laden.

Now, take time to **note the baking and food items that you intend to make for your family's use and as gifts** this year.

53

CHRISTMAS BAKING & FOOD PREPARATION:

AMT.	ITEM	PURPOSE	RECIPE REF'NCE	TIME PERIOD	When Trans.
3	ging'bread houses	for gifts	cards	Dec 13-20	✓
4	dark fruit cakes	2-us., 2-gifts	Joy 'Cooking p91	Nov 1-7	✓
+batches	caramel corn	ourselves	cards	Dec 5-12	

Note each food item and the quantity you plan to make on this planning sheet. Also list the purpose (for your own consumption or for gifts) and where the recipe is kept. Indicate a time period for the completion of each item. Some goodies need to be made and served while fresh; others can be done ahead and frozen until needed. Fruitcake, for example, needs to be baked about six to eight weeks ahead since it improves in flavor as it ages. Include on this planning sheet the items for your Christmas dinner or for any entertaining that can be made ahead. The "Time Period" column in the sample planning sheet indicates the day or days at which you have plugged the item into your calendar. At this point you can begin to see whether this part of Christmas preparation is proportionate to your available time. You may need to eliminate some items if time gets too short.

As you plan your Christmas baking and entertaining, review your recipes and **make a shopping list of ingredients. Purchase these ingredients early while supplies are plentiful or on sale,** perhaps a few with each shopping trip to avoid strain on the December food budget. Try to do your shopping during the time of day when the stores are less crowded. Even on Saturday, if you go shopping as soon as the stores open you have a better selection of fresh produce and you don't have to battle the

54

55 crowds that appear later in the day. **Take an inventory of your freezer, refrigerator, and pantry so that you** will know what you have on hand and save money by avoiding duplicate purchases. You will probably want to **have enough quick-meal supplies on hand for at least two meals.** Unexpected guests might drop in or you may even find your own family caught short one day when you are delayed. Canned ham and chicken make good emergency supplies, plus canned vegetables and a biscuit mix, along with a frozen dessert.

56 In November, as you make your regular meals, **mix double batches of main dishes and freeze a portion to be used in December** when the pressure is on. Good make-ahead dishes include soups, meatballs, casseroles, cakes, pies, and so on. What about trying to make at least one double batch of something each week so that each week in December you can have one instant-preparation meal? Also take a few minutes to plan everyday family meals during the month of December; it may be the difference between sinking and staying afloat. It will be worth the time and effort once you have done this. The following year you could use the same menu, making only minor changes—a gift to yourself from last Christmas.

Baking

57 If possible, **do some of your holiday baking in November.** Fruit or vegetable loaves of cranberry, carrot, lemon, date-nut, pumpkin, pineapple, banana, and zucchini make good eating and freeze well. Try making them in mini-tins for older or single friends and give them a variety of two or three types of

bread. Wrap the loaves in plastic wrap and then in aluminum foil, and tape an artificial Christmas flower or sprig of holly on top with a ribbon tied around it for an attractive and thoughtful gift.

Cookies make excellent gifts and can be made far ahead and frozen until ready for use. Try making gingerbread or sugar cookies in different shapes, decorating with icing, and then arranging them on a paper plate with plastic wrap on top. If you want your cookies to be hung on a tree, break a toothpick in half and insert a piece in the dough after it has been cut out and placed on the cookie sheet. Bake the cookies with the toothpicks still inserted and leave them there until the cookies are cool. You now have a ready-made hole in which to thread a ribbon for hanging the cookies on the tree after they have been decorated. Cookie cutters are available for gingerbread men, women, boys, and girls, so you could make a whole gingerbread family for giving to a favorite neighbor on your gift list. For an extra-personal touch, place the name or initial of each individual on the cookie with frosting while you are decorating. If you need to store the cookies for a few days, hide them under your children's beds—they will never find them!. . . . if you don't have house pets.

Join a cookie exchange. Consider baking an extra-large batch of your favorite cookie recipe. For example, bake twelve dozen and arrange with five friends to do the same, and swap two dozen of your favorites for two dozen of each of theirs. This gives each of you twelve dozen cookies in six varieties, saving lots of work.

Although jellies, jams, pickles, and relishes aren't baked items, they, too, can be prepared in the fall for Christmas sharing.

Christmas Entertaining

58 **For entertaining, make a time schedule, plan the menu ahead, and post it so you don't forget to prepare or purchase any of the necessary items.** Give yourself time before the day of the party to prepare some of the menu foods such as set-salads, rolls, and dessert so that everything doesn't have to be fixed on party day. On the day of the dinner, write out a time line, going backward from the serving hour, to make it all happen:

9:00 AM	Prepare dressing.
10:00 AM	Start turkey.
11:00 AM	Vacuum and dust eating area.
Noon	Set table and arrange chairs.
1:30 PM	Peel potatoes and carrots and cover with water.
2:30 PM	Start Christmas pudding steaming.
2:45 PM	Put cranberries, pickles, and butter into dishes.
3:00 PM	Start potatoes and carrots cooking.
3:30 PM	Take turkey out of oven and warm rolls.
3:45 PM	Make gravy and carve turkey (get help); put water and ice in drinking glasses.
4:00 PM	Eat dinner.

59 Some people love to entertain during the holidays. If you aren't one of these, go to the parties you are invited to and enjoy yourself, but **don't feel obligated by the "I have to have a party, too" syndrome,** because you *don't* have to have one, especially not at this season of the year. Entertaining should be something that you look forward to, not dread. If it's a big hassle for you, then wait until you feel more like doing it, perhaps in July.

If you do wish to entertain during this festive season, keep it simple! **Buffet dinners are simpler than the sit-down type, and a potluck party where everyone brings something is even easier.** One group has parties often, but the friends have made a pact within the group that every party is a potluck type. They vary the menu to keep it interesting. The hostess and host determine which type of party they wish to have, for example, one with Chinese food. As they call to invite everyone, they describe the menu, and the guests decide what they would like to bring. Another month it might be an Italian-food evening. During the hot summer months each friend takes a salad and his or her own steak to barbecue, and the hostess supplies baked potatoes and garlic bread. This idea makes for easy entertaining—easy on the hostess and easy on the guests, as well as on the budgets.

Not all functions need to be held within a twelve-day radius of Christmas. **If you are in charge of setting the date, consider spreading some of the recitals, plays, parties, and programs through the fall and spring months.** For a large extended family, it may be more convenient to have a get-together several weeks before Christmas or the week after, reserving Christmas Day for immediate families at home. Again, let the other families contribute something toward the menu to make it easy on the host and hostess. The Cooper family likes to get together with Grandma and Grandpa and all the aunts, uncles, and cousins, but their extended family is so large that they can't possibly do it in one home. So they rent a community facility for the afternoon and have a dinner in the first part of December. The dinner is coordinated by one of the families and a second family is in charge of entertainment, which includes games, prizes, and shared talents. Each family takes a few minutes to highlight its accomplishments during the past year. This idea could be extended further by writing the accomplishments down and giving them to Grandma and Grandpa along with pictures and photocopies of certificates and awards earned by family members, placing these in a looseleaf album to be treasured. (Can you think of a nicer Christmas gift?) A reunion keeps the extended family united and is looked forward to throughout the year. Santa could make a surprise visit during the evening with small gifts for the children. The Coopers' reunion includes singing carols and everyone helps to clean up, making a pleasant family tradition without too much work for anyone.

Entertaining Children

62 **If you are entertaining children during the holiday season, their food, activities, and entertainment need to be well planned and executed.** Keep the food simple so you will have time to be *with* children rather than hustling in the kitchen. For teens, a potluck party works well, with everyone bringing something to put on the pizza or a favorite snack (pickles, chips, or soft drinks) to go with chili burgers, hamburgers, hobo sandwiches, or whatever you choose to serve as your main course. Plan on some type of entertainment for the children at their party. Hire a puppeteer, rent a video, take them tobogganing or roller skating. Children are all pretty excited at this time of year so plan ahead. Play some active group games such as floor hockey at the local school gymnasium, volleyball, or quiet games in your home. Check the library or bookstore for books with party themes and games. There's no need to keep the children all day; just a couple of hours is enough to make them feel like they've had a good time and it is often long enough for the host or hostess as well.

A popular party activity that children love is decorating cookies or small cakes, or building graham-cracker houses. Wearing aprons and chef's caps adds to the fun. (Buy paper aprons and caps at a restaurant-supply store.) Have prepared bowls of colored frosting and decorating condiments. Another well-liked party activity is making ornaments and decorations. Have the supplies ready for the children to make a simple project they can take home when the party is over. The activity could be to make a gift for their parent; or you could sponsor a "Santa's Workshop" party where kids make something for residents in a rest home or shelter.

December birthdays are one type of entertaining that should not be avoided. Bev Cooper explains, "We have a son whose birthday is Christmas Eve, and we always felt it was important to make that a special day for him, not because it was easy, but because it was *his* special day and it should not be postponed or substituted for another day. After all, it wasn't his fault that he was born on the day before Christmas, and he shouldn't be penalized by not being allowed to celebrate as other children do. We always had a birthday party for him and found that it did not make a big difference to our Christmas preparations. We made him a cake of his choice, but we did use Christmas decorations as our theme and Christmas trinkets as favors. Because the house was usually already decorated it really wasn't a big deal to sponsor a party. This birthday was carefully separated from Christmas Day and we never allowed ourselves to combine birthday and Christmas gifts, so our son didn't feel cheated in that way either. Birthday gifts were wrapped in traditional birthday paper always."

Welcome to Our Home

Whenever you entertain, and whether your guests are adults or children or both, create a warm atmosphere. Get your house smelling Christmasy by boiling some water with a little cinnamon or cloves in it. There's no need to explain when you don't serve something spicy, but the house will smell great. An easy way to create a beautiful atmosphere for your adult entertaining is to light a fire, dim the lights, and put on some soft Christmas music. Bake something sweet or yeasty for lunch so the house fills with that special smell, simple and effective. You can also buy potpourri, scented candles or spray fragrances in holiday scents.

A hot, spiced cider drink served with toasted almonds makes a real treat. A cheese ball and crackers also makes a nice nibble, as do caramel corn, a dried-fruit mix, or a cereal-and-nut party snack. Banana slush is a tasty drink—always ready to serve when friends drop in as long as you keep some ginger ale on hand to mix with it (see recipes in the "Last Bite" chapter).

Last but not least, work at keeping the living room straightened up. This is the time of year for entertaining—preplanned or drop-in. Be prepared so that no matter what the day, the hour, or the age of your guests, *you're* not caught short by having an untidy living room or by not having some snack or meal that can be served if you choose without advance notice.

5th Bite—Decorating the House and the Tree

From the planning calendar, you already know the target date for having the decorations up. To some people decorating means redoing the whole house; to others it means just putting up a tree and a few garlands. If it is now late in the season, set your target date, put up the things you have, and forget about adornments you hoped to create. Make decorating the tree or your home a pleasant experience. If you have young children, plan something constructive to keep them busy (they love to make paper chains) while you are checking out the lights and fastening them to the tree; otherwise, the kids will be into everything while you're hassling with the lights. Put on some Christmas music for atmosphere and enjoy a treat afterward.

Most of us make or acquire decorations and ornaments a few at a time, each becoming a part of our tradition, bringing sentimental value. But realize that just because you followed a certain motif for your tree or had your decorations around for ten years doesn't mean that you must keep using them forever. If you would enjoy a change, then by all means make some changes. If you have too many decorations and find that your home looks cluttered, or if it takes a long time to put them all up and take them down again, discard those that have no meaning or that don't look nice anymore and set aside part of the other decorations to be rotated. One year you might want a red-and-white tree and the next year a blue-and-silver one. The main thing is that your home and your Christmas decor reflect the personality of your family and create the atmosphere you wish to nurture.

When you would like to change your theme or add to what you already have, set up a tentative plan. If it is early in the year, you may have time to make some of your new decorations. **Write down the ornaments or decorations you wish to make or purchase for the future.** You'll get more of the effect you want if you have a overall plan, rather than buying decorations on impulse. One woman said, "I like to add one new long-lasting decoration each year. Two years ago it was a manger scene; last year we bought a stained-glass star. Now we are beginning to buy pieces for a village to go on the mantel." It is fun to dream, look, and plan, adding to the sentimental value of your decorating theme.

63

Decorating Ideas

If a pinecone wreath is your goal, why not make it in October when the cones are plentiful and gather your own instead of purchasing them from a craft shop or garden center. Also gather dried weeds and nuts to be included in your wreath. A pinecone wreath is an elegant decoration and is another item that would be treasured and appreciated if you were to make an extra one as a gift for a special person on your list. Wreaths are simple to make (inquire at a craft supply store or at your local library for directions), inexpensive, and easily stored for several years of use.

Making new Christmas stockings can be a fun project. It doesn't cost much to make giant stockings from red fake-fur fabric. Just draw a pattern on newspaper, making sure it is large enough to get your hand into the hole after the seams are stitched. The fur fabric will not ravel and it is washable. A more time-consuming project, but a very rewarding one, is to make fancy stockings—needlepoint, knitted, crocheted, or sewn with felt, sequins, and trims. Match the hobby or interest of the person for whom the stocking is made, such as a cowboy boot for a young cowpoke; a ballet slipper for an aspiring ballerina; a gum boot for a fisherman; a fashion boot for a stylish young lady; a roller skate, tennis shoe, or sport sock for an athlete; a jogging shoe for a runner; and a mukluk, ski boot, or hockey or figure skate for a winter-sports fan. Let your imagination and their personal interests take over. Stockings also make good gifts for newlyweds and they can be as simple or elegant as you wish them to be. Be prepared, however, for the youngsters might still prefer to hang up the old bedraggled ones for Santa to fill and just use the new ones to decorate the fireplace. (Stocking-filler ideas are mentioned under "Plain and Fancy Traditions.") Stockings can be personalized with initials or names and they can be large or mini-sized to hang on a tree or display in a bedroom. They can be knitted, appliquéd, or plain. Everyone enjoys this time-tested and decorative symbol of Christmas.

The stocking tradition need not stop when youngsters become Santa-wise. Parents could continue to fill the stockings or children might begin taking part by putting small gift items in the stockings of other family members, including Mom and Dad. You decide what fits your needs. McCulloughs chose to quit filling stockings for their children when they had all passed twelve. The cost of filling a stocking with goodies and trinkets for teens became very expensive and still wasn't that significant to them.

If you would like a Christmas tablecloth but the prices are prohibitive, why not dye a white bedsheet red or green, add a smaller lace cloth that will cover the center of the colored cloth, and place your centerpiece, candles, or punchbowl on the lace. Another idea is to give close friends red and green felt-tip pens or tube fabric paints when they visit, to autograph a white sheet precut to the size you want for your dining room table. Add lace, if you like, to the tablecloth to make it even more attractive. Napkin-sized pieces might be cut out and given to each guest for their signatures as well.

Display your Christmas cards as part of your home decoration. Put up a string along a wall to hang them on; attach ribbon streamers to the top of the door; or cut a tree shape from felt or fabric and mount it on a door. Then pin your cards onto the tree as you receive them. Cover a door with foil or Christmas wrap and tape the cards on for an easy, attractive display. Use a wicker basket with a bow or sprig of artificial greenery to be your card receptacle.

Make a candy wreath for your door or entryway. Use an 8-inch macramé ring or bend a metal coat hanger to form a circle. Wrap the ring with ribbon to cover it and tie a piece of ribbon about 12 inches long to the top of the ring. Knot a pair of kindergarten scissors to the other end of the ribbon. Attach as many wrapped candies as possible all around the ring, using strong thread, string, or fine wire. Add a bow and a sprig of artificial greenery to the top of the wreath to make it look more attractive. As guests leave your home, they can cut off and enjoy a piece of candy.

Decorations and tree ornaments can be made from toilet-paper rolls, egg cartons, clothespins, ribbon, pom-poms, and so on. Hundreds of ideas are available in magazines, books, boutiques, and craft shops.

An especially attractive tree ornament can be made at very little cost by covering a 3-inch styrofoam ball with fabric scraps cut into 1½-inch squares, so that when it is finished the ball appears to have been stuffed and quilted. Using a metal fingernail file or a dull tableknife, poke all four edges of a calico cloth square into the ball. Take another piece and place it next to the first one and poke that edge into the same slit. Continue filling in the entire surface of the ball. Then fold a 6-inch piece of ribbon in half and with glue or a pin secure the cut ends to the ball so the ornament can be hung. A lollipop tree ornament can be made by poking a 5-inch dowel (3/16 inch in diameter) halfway into a styrofoam ball (1½ inch diameter). Cut a 7-inch circle out of calico-print fabric with pinking shears.

Wrap the ball with calico, and secure and tie a bow at the base of the ball with narrow ribbon about 10 inches long. To make a hanger, use a needle and a piece of clear fishing line.

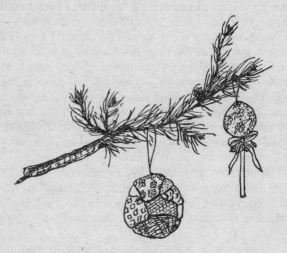

6th Bite—Christmas is for Kids, Too!

It is often said, "Christmas is for children," but sometimes we wish they would wait quietly on a chair and just show up serenely on Christmas morning. That will not happen, and what's more, children may misbehave, not even responding to threats that "Santa won't come." A better solution is to **look for ways to let the children be a part of your preparations.** Assign one to be in charge of displaying cards on the door or wall or banister—wherever you put them. Children love sealing envelopes and licking stamps. Let the children take part in getting ready—decorating the tree, making gifts, baking cookies, sending cards, breaking nuts, learning songs and poems. Try to **maintain a reasonable routine for children including regular bedtimes, naps when appropriate, and sit-down meals.** Make sure you and they eat nutritious meals, avoiding too many sugary foods.

As the final day draws nearer, build a climax by allowing more time to be with your children, because they need extra help passing the time and managing their feelings of excitement and anticipation. Picking a compassionate service project that your children can take part in will also help the time pass quickly, and it will draw their attention away from "What am I getting?" to the fun of giving.

Much more on this topic is discussed in the chapter entitled "Spreading Goodwill Toward Men," with special focus on drawing close to grandparents.

Waiting It Out—Making the Waiting Easier

Don't torment young children by setting gifts under the tree too early. Waiting is hard for children. Often they don't even comprehend how long a week is. Most families use some sort of Advent calendar to count the days until Christmas. Some include a special little activity for the child to do each day such as fixing hot chocolate or making snowmen out of marshmallows and toothpicks. Following are several variations on the Advent calendar. If you have more than one child, they could take turns using the calendar. This ritual can take place at breakfast time or after dinner. If you are so inclined, you can include a devotion time by reading a poem, a short story, or Scripture and singing a carol.

1. Cut strips of colored paper to link together in a chain calendar. Each day one loop can be torn off to show how many more tomorrows until Christmas. A special color could indicate the passing of a week, such as white links for Sundays. To go even further with this idea, inside each link write something for the family to do together such as singing a favorite carol, reading a certain Christmas story, baking cookies, or driving around your neighborhood and seeing the lights.
2. For an inexpensive Advent calendar use a December calendar. Buy Christmas stickers or cut

up old Christmas cards, one for each day until Christmas, and put them in an envelope. Then each day, have the children put a sticker or a figure from the envelope on the right square of the calendar.

3. You can buy or make a picture-window Advent calendar on which a window is opened each day. Some specialty shops carry the kind with chocolates hidden beneath twenty-five doors.

4. Create your own long-lasting Advent wall hanging. The basics include a fabric background with a painted or appliquéd tree, twenty-five numbered pockets at the bottom, and twenty-five trinket surprises to be put in the pockets along with a method of mounting these on the calendar background. Each day one item is taken from the appropriate pocket and attached to the tree.

5. If you have a ceramic or wooden nativity scene as part of your decorations, put one piece out each night, explaining its role in the Christmas story. On Christmas morning put the baby Jesus in the manger to bring your family's thoughts around to the real meaning of the day.

We can truly make the Christmas season special if we prepare wisely and well. Often we can take the time to set up a tradition that can be used over and over again like the permanent Advent calendar. The McCulloughs painted a green tree on a piece of wood and framed it. Bonnie pounded twenty-five little gold nails on the tree. Twenty-five more nails were used to hang tiny ornaments around the base of the tree. When all the ornaments are hung on the tree, it is Christmas Day. The family has been using the same simple Advent display for many years.

Another mother took a three-ring notebook titled it "The Hansen Christmas Scrapbook," and let the kids glue wrapping paper and card motifs all over the cover, mosaic-fashion. When the children were small, they put favorite cards or school drawings about Christmas in it. Mom collected stories for the book, some humorous ones like "Kermit's Christmas Diary" from *Woman's Day* magazine, and some faith-promoting and touching stories such as "Twelve Christmas Miracles That Really Happened" from *Family Circle* magazine. As the children grew older, they too watched for special pictures, clippings, and snapshots to add. Just having a child look through the pages can give Mom time to get dinner on the table. The scrapbook became a permanent part of the Hansens' traditions and it has now expanded to several volumes.

A variation on keeping the scrapbook is to make an ABC book for the young child using a page for each letter of the alphabet and putting in pictures from old Christmas cards or drawing original pictures. A line for each page could be included—"A is for Angels with white robes so bright; they told shepherds of Jesus' birth that first Christmas night." Older children could help put this together for younger brothers, sisters, or cousins.

Involve your children in the ornament and decoration projects whenever possible. Children usually make these at school and bring them home. If they aren't what you want for your tree, cut a tree shape out of green poster paper and mount it on the back of the child's bedroom door. Then let the child make decorations for "his" or "her" tree! Purchase a styrofoam cane and tape red ribbon around it to resemble the stripes in a candy cane. Attach ribbon streamers to hang from the cane and give one of your children the responsibility of pinning the Christmas cards that you receive to the ribbon streamers so they can be displayed. Mount the cane on a wall or door in a horizontal position so the streamers can be easily reached by the child.

Plan Some Things To Do

The last seven days are the hardest of all for children. They are excited and sometimes frustrated. They want to be a part of everything. As Christmas Day draws closer, recognize that the little ones will need more and more adult association. Give some thought to activities they can do at home, because you can't take them places and entertain them all the time. We all think of letting children help make cookies, but that creates such a mess that most parents don't take on the project more than once a year. **Have a few craft projects in mind for the children to do while you are busy.** Libraries and bookstores have hundreds of activity and craft books from which to glean ideas. If this is an emergency and the Christmas shelf at the library is empty, we mention a few activities here to get you started.

Remember, your friends are feeling the same pressures, and their children are also experiencing hyperactivity. Maybe you can swap children. Get together with three friends, and each afternoon the children can go to a different home for lunch and activities such as skating, sledding, baking, craft making, or just playing. Each mother has three free afternoons and one hectic one.

Keep a box of doodads to be used for craft projects. Collect such things as cotton balls, beads, buttons, trinkets, gummed stickers, rubber stamps, stars, yarn, a glue stick, paper clips, toothpicks, and pieces of ribbon, lace, or rick-rack trims. The new puffy paints and glitter glues are wonderfully fun.

1. **Make chains.** Cut strips of paper to be looped together, each fastened with tape or staples (glue takes too long to set and keeps popping open). Kids love any project where they can use lots of tape. The chains can be draped on the tree, a long stairway, or in the child's bedroom.

2. **Teach children to cut paper snowflakes.** They love to hang them everywhere. They are made like the stars you learned to cut in grade school. Fold a piece of paper in half, then fold on top of first fold two times until you have a skinny triangle. Cut out little notches along both edges. Open up and be surprised by a different design each time. You can save several folding steps by using white paper napkins to make snowflakes.

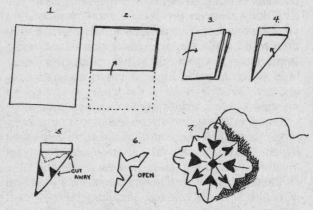

3. **Let your children make Christmas placemats.** They could be reusable if covered with clear contact paper. Use any kind of paper; you can buy plain paper matts at the grocery or party store. Let the kids create designs with stencils or patterns, decorate with stick-ons, or color with crayons and paints.

4. Stringing popcorn and cranberries is an old-fashioned method of keeping children occupied as well as decorating the tree. For greater success use large-kernel popcorn (air popper makes big kernels), a darning needle and dental floss for thread. A faster project for younger children is to thread large items like various pastas, bits of styrofoam packing, buttons, beads, and short pieces of drinking straws. Try an eatable garland by stringing cereal such Cheerios or Fruit Loops, and candy pieces like licorice. String pretzels together by weaving a narrow ribbon in-and-out of the pretzel holes. Simple, cute and kids love it!

5. Stencils are popular. Buy from the delightful selection of metal templates now on the market or cut your own stencil from a file folder with a sharp knife. Dip a sponge or stiff brush into a little paint and decorate paper items or fabric apron, tote-bag, t-shirt or canvas shoes.

6. Make gift tags for packages or placecards. These could be cut from last year's cards and hole-punched for ribbon. If you don't have any old cards, use colored construction paper and stencils.

7. Kids love to be creative with ink pads and stamps. Make your own stamps. No need to carve a carrot or potato, just use a piece of thin foam, like the Dr. Scholl's products found in the foot department of the drugstore. Draw a simple figure or word on the paper backing, cut it out, peel it off, and stick the foam to a little block of wood. Presto, you're ready to dab the stamp on an ink pad and start decorating paper for wrap or cards. Pads are now readily available with water soluable ink for easy cleanup.

8. Cut out paper garlands with simple shapes of angels, trees, stars, bells, children, etc.

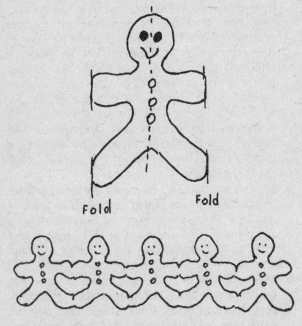

Fold   Fold

9. Let kids make wrapping paper for family members by drawing and coloring pictures on white butcher paper or plain brown wrapping paper. They can also use a rubber stamp to decorate plain paper, even if it only has your name and address on it.

10. Have just as much fun as making cookies without the flour mess by allowing the kids to trace around the cookie-cutter shapes on paper, thin foam sheets, or felt.

11. Make an orange-juice-can or soda-pop-can pencil holder or penny bank, or decorate a gift

box by cutting small pieces of wrapping paper, card motifs, sticky contact paper, or wallpaper to cover it.

12. Decorate lollipop cookies (bake sugar cookies with popsicle sticks inserted before baking). Using Q-tips, paint them with colored egg yolk before baking. Make them look like faces by using the right color for hair, eyes, and so on.

13. To help your home smell good for the holidays, give children some oranges and a box of whole cloves to press into the fruit. Hang by a ribbon to spread the spicy smell throughout the various rooms or put the pomander balls in a bowl.

14. Use glitter, glue, and yarn on pinecones to make attractive ornaments.

15. Make puppets from paper lunch bags and color with crayons, markers, or pencils.

16. Paint round rocks to make crazy critters.

17. Make Salt Clay: 1 Cup Table salt, 1 Cup Flour, 1/2 cup cold water and a touch of food coloring or paint. Mix ingredients and knead well. Store in a plastic bag in the refrigerator until you need it. Let the kids use it like clay and roll into snakes and make all kinds of shapes. They can make decorations by rolling it out like cookies, poke a hole in the top of the cookie with a straw, let shapes dry flat, then paint. Can later be sprayed with for a shiny finish. Tie a ribbon in the hole.

18. Use a large piece of butcher or brown wrapping paper and let the child make a "Big as Life" poster of himself. Spread the paper on the floor and have the child lie down. Have an adult trace around the child's body with crayon or marker. The child can color in the person to be himself, an astronaut, nurse, etc. Then cut out and hang from string or tape to a wall.

The Right Gift for Your Child

You won't win every time, but with practice, evaluation, and planning, you can improve your gift-giving success. You love your child, and you want to give the right kind of gift. You probably have memories of some toys that broke on the first day, and others that were hardly touched. You keep hunting for just the right gift that your child will like and that will help develop creativity and self-confidence. Ask yourself these questions as you consider your list: Is the gift beyond the child's physical or mental ability? Is it safe? How many batteries does it take and how often will they need to be replaced? Will it stimulate imagination, skills, or creativity? How much will the child use it, compared to the cost investment? Might it break easily? Does it need to be assembled? Can you manage that assembly? TV commercials have a strong influence on children's wants and desires. Prepare children for a gentle letdown if those desires won't be fulfilled. None of us has everything we want; help the child learn to handle such a circumstance.

For gift ideas, read through toy suggestions in parenting books for enlightenment as to the right type of toy for your child's developmental stage. Keeping a year-round idea list as suggested in the chapter "Gifts and Giving" will help. **Think about an overall gift plan.** For example, if you give your six-year-old his own radio this year, what will there be left to give him when he is ten—a CD player? Will there be anything left for him to want when he is fourteen? Some parents have found it very helpful to have a general idea of when various types of gifts will be given—sort of a master plan—and to try not to force the child to grow up too soon. At what age do you think it is proper for a child to be given a bicycle? Radio? Watch? Tape recorder? CD player?

Grandpa Runyan gives each of his grandchildren a watch on their eighth birthday. They all know it and the anticipation is great. Another man, who delights in woodworking, presents his granddaughters with a cedar chest at age sixteen. He has rifles for the boys only *after* they have passed the hunters' safety course. A mother who lives in a big city says it is too dangerous for little children to have their own bicycles until they are at least eight, mature enough to better understand traffic rules. She doesn't let the children have radios until after age thirteen, when they are interested in news and modern music—radio broadcasting is not directed to the young child. However, she makes sure that every five-year-old has access to beginning reading and picture books. They also have enjoyed a record player or simple tape recorder for juvenile songs and stories. Put some thought into the needs and level of development of your child. Give gifts that help build self-confidence. And that doesn't necessarily mean just educational toys. Playing is good for children. Many play toys help children with language skills and problem solving. Your selection of gifts can help youngsters have a variety of play experiences, some using big muscles, some for quiet play, some involving other children and developing social skills, and others increasing creative and artistic talents. A trampoline that uses excess energy might be worth the investment.

Gifts don't always have to be expensive or new. 68 There are times when you pay dearly for a box yet the items inside don't add up to the cost. Calculate the cost of putting together the supplies for your own kits. Put in yarn, knitting needles, and instructions along with a note promising help if needed.

Give youngsters original kits. A magnifying glass, microscope, slides, butterfly net, and other items make up a "Discovery Kit." Make a "Dress-up Box" for little children by collecting old pieces of jewelry, hats, purses, a mirror, shoes, wigs, and powder puffs. There are many possibilities; just use your imagination: doctor's kit, nurse's kit, first-aid kit, stamp-collecting kit, artist's kit, sculptor's kit, cookie-making kit, or tool box. Use sturdy boxes that can be labeled and decorated to create a kit as nice as any you could buy.

A child loves to receive a whole package of paper all to himself or herself with pencils, markers, blunt scissors, tape, stick-ons, and rub-on letters. Have you thought of a rubber stamp with the child's name on it and an ink pad? Children love to have their own stationery, especially with their own name. Wrap a tiny toy or candy treat with yards of colorful yarn or string. Attach notes every few yards with expressions of love or appreciation, jokes, or hints about the surprise in the center. Give a child a treasure box full of costume jewelry. Children love to receive their own plants, even fuzzy cacti. What about a cut-glass prism to be hung in the window to cast rainbows on their walls? Older kids might enjoy a bike pump, a backpack, a pedometer, or posters to decorate their walls. They also appreciate receiving status T-shirts from various colleges or universities, and shirts with humorous sayings.

Help Your Child Get Organized

Children enjoy their toys, books, collections, and clothes more if they are organized. You are doing them a favor if you **help your kids organize the bed-room and playroom and then periodically go back with them to keep these things in order.** If a child's bedroom is constantly a mess, it is a pretty sure sign that the room has more contents than the child can manage. **Store part of the toys, games, and clothes elsewhere to be rotated.** Give away some of the excess. Let the children be a part of these decisions and they will learn managing skills. They are more likely to take proper care of their things, and the toys and clothes will last longer, which could mean quite a money savings. Children should be taught the proper way of "picking up". . . . putting blocks in the bucket, crayons in a box, rather than all dumped together.

For further instruction on helping your child clean and organize the bedroom, read Bonnie McCullough and Susan Monson's book, *401 Ways to Get Your Kids to Work at Home* ($8.95, St. Martin's Press). Remember that hooks, shelves, and little bags and boxes make better organizers than large toy boxes in which everything is dumped. The approaching holiday is a good motivator to get the children to weed out the games, toys, books, and clothes that aren't used. These items can be stored for a younger brother or sister or donated to a charity.

Some time ago, Bonnie McCullough and Tammy Radich sponsored a "Children's Shopping Day." Parents donated handcrafted items, and the children shopped. They loved it. The gifts were lovely and it was so successful that the group will probably do it again. The instruction sheet and sign-up form is shown in case you should like to start a gift exchange co-op with your friends.

The gift exchange (kids called it the gift giveaway)

was a terrific success. We found most kids forgot to bring a bag, but we had taken grocery sacks just in case. We were shortest on gifts for men. The little children went crazy over some of the items because they were things they wanted for themselves, but later they got back to thinking of people on their gift lists. Because we had no more than thirty families participate, it ended up that the parents usually helped their own young ones—so what does it matter if Mom or Dad knows what her or his own gift is? There wasn't really any clean-up; we all just helped put the tables away. We were smart not to have refreshments.

Because we had no deadline, parents kept dropping in and out of the project when their lives got too busy. Even a $2.00 entry fee would have made a more definite commitment, but we had to keep it totally nonprofit, with no money exchanged, to use the church building. We held it to a strict swap operation, avoiding any price marking or comparing of relative values.

Gift suggestions: aprons, dish towels, stick horses, stationery, pincushions, eyeglass holders, shaving-gear bags, jewelry boards, spice ropes, magnets, recipe holders, keychains, beanbags, potted plants, preserves, candy, puppets, plaques, pomanders, sachets, dolls, balls, wind chimes, fancy boxes, ceramics, knitted or crocheted items, puzzles, pencil holders, games, stuffed animals, rock people, pajama bags, macramé items, sewing kits, keyholders, wood items, paperweights, pretty soaps, banks, pillows, trivets, clotheshangers, and hair ornaments.

Children's Gift Exchange Co-op

You, as a parent, are invited to join the Children's Gift Exchange Co-op. The purpose is to provide a way for children to do their Christmas shopping without a great deal of expense. To enter your child, between the ages of three and eleven, the parent will make and donate seven handcrafted items (all alike), worth between $2.50 and $5.00 each (retail value) for each child who takes part. We expect good-quality items that the children can be proud to give, not just quick crafts. This is a totally nonprofit project. The advantages of this program are that the children have a nice selection of gifts to choose from and have a pleasant shopping experience, and the parents can make items that they know how to make (perhaps last year's specialty). Each child will have an opportunity to pick out and take home seven gifts from the display.

Please name the item you will make so we'll know whether all areas are covered. Gifts will be needed for younger and older brothers and sisters, Moms and Dads, and grandparents. We are trying to stay away from ornaments and concentrate more on personal gifts.

Date of exchange: *Submit this form to:*
Date _____   Name _____
Time _____   Address _____
Place _____   Phone _____

Parent's Name _____ Phone _____
Address _____
Child's name _____ Age _____
Describe gift item you plan to make suitable for (circle):
Toddler Girl Boy Teen-girl Teen-boy
Adult-female Adult-male

7th Bite—Spreading Goodwill Toward Men

The Christmas season is a good time to nurture the value of service to others. It turns hearts away from commercialism and "What will I get?" to "How can I help someone else?" You can work on building relationships with grandparents, extended family, and "adopted" family, or on providing anonymous service to those in need. Thoughts and successful suggestions are offered for each of these areas.

Extended Family, Especially Grandparents

Children who have a loving relationship with their grandparents are lucky indeed, because both gain an important sense of belonging by associating with each other. Children can learn to enjoy the past and appreciate their heritage by looking at family pictures with their grandparents and by listening to the experiences of the older generation. They can feel proud of the accomplishments of their elders and empathize with their hardships. Children want to know their roots, learning that what we have today is built on what others did in the past. It is worthwhile for parents to make it possible for their children to get together with their grandparents; however, not all grandparents are willing or able to play a loving and supportive role in their grandchildren's lives. If this is the case, accept the situation by helping the child love beyond circumstance and keep in contact as much as possible. If it is not appropriate to use your parents as an avenue to **build second-generation relationships,** include someone else—an aunt, uncle, older neighbor, or church member, or adopt grandparents from your local rest home. It is important for children to know that others besides their parents care for them. Grandparents or other caring adults can often give back-up support and individual attention. Children need someone to "oooh" and "aaah" over them, to give warm hugs, to care, to give positive compliments about small accomplishments that the Big World doesn't notice.

Following is a collection of fun ideas we have gathered that can be adapted to your family. We have also included some activities for grandparents to do. If you don't have grandchildren, you can focus on a child who will benefit from your tender gestures. No one will be using all these ideas, this is a buffet of choices. Keep in mind that there comes a time when grandparents can no longer give as much to the younger generation because of the number of children or their own failing health, but they still need to *receive* your love and attention. Great-grandpa Runyan is eighty-seven; he has six children, thirty-six grandchildren, 108 great-grandchildren and one great-great-grandchild. He is long beyond giving each grandchild a new ornament every Christmas, but he always offers a peppermint and stops to show off the wall of posterity pictures.

Gift Ideas for Children to Give to Grandparents

- Make a birthday calendar showing all children's, spouses', and grandchildren's anniversaries and birth dates. Buy a pretty calendar and write in these special dates and decorate with colorful stickers. Or make a permanent birthday board with twelve blocks, one for each month, listing the dates and names in the appropriate squares.

- Personalize a calendar by replacing the art with photos of your family or use the children's art work.

- Send a monthly letter. Establish a traditional chain letter, with each family adding to the envelope within a week and sending it on to the next family and so on until it reaches the grandparents.

- Audio or video tape-record a message at Christmas with each of the children speaking or performing something on tape. Even the gurgles of a new baby make grandparents feel closer. Be sure to tell all the Christmas happenings that are going on, including what is happening at school, home, and church. These are precious to far-away grandparents who miss out on so much of the everyday lives of their families, and it helps the children feel closer to them, too.

- Give toy gifts and games to Grandma and Grandpa so that the children can play with them when they visit their home.

- Make dishtowels or placemats by having each of your children draw a picture on a piece of white paper with transfer pencils. Iron these original works of art onto permanent-press or plain quilted fabric. Color them with liquid paints, and finish off the fabric edges. You can also purchase fabric crayons at a craft store. Let each child draw a picture with the crayons, then iron the picture onto the cloth—it *is* washable, but it cannot be put in the dryer or bleached. Still another variation is to make a quilt by ironing the designs from washable crayons, or transferring the children's pictures onto a flat bed sheet and painting with liquid paints. Use a matching sheet for the back, place batting in between, tie with yarn knots at set intervals to keep the batting in place, tuck in the outside edges, and stitch closed.

- Give grandparents a tree ornament with the baby's picture on it as each grandchild joins the family.

- Make felt ornaments by tracing around the child's hand, cutting two felt copies, stitching the edges closed, and stuffing lightly. Put the child's name and date on it.

- Arrange for each child and grandchild to send one tulip bulb for grandparents' garden.

- Design a wall grouping of family pictures and hang it for Grandma and Grandpa.

- Folks who live alone on a fixed income probably would be delighted to receive a basket of goodies: small cans of salmon, chicken, ham, tuna, vegetables, fruit, instant coffee, crackers, cheese, cookies and instant soup mixes. Or, they might appreciate a box of all-occasion cards, postcards, stationery, stamps and writing pen. Recycle a basket by spray painting it to contain your shower of helpful gifts.

- Have children touch hand or feet to colorful acrylic paint and decorate a tea-towel, apron or pillow case with their prints. Kids need help with this one. Let only one child at a time do this project. Use a throw-away pie tin for paint; wear old clothes; have rags handy and wash up immediately.

- Let your children send a homemade card made especially for grandparents.

- Make a family tree picture by drawing or stitching the silhouette of a tree. Put family pictures on it— parents on the trunk and children in the branches. You can even show three generations—grandparents on trunk, children as branches, grandchildren in outer foliage.

- Consider gifts that give more than once, such as flowers delivered every month, tickets to a concert or play series, magazine subscription, or cords of firewood.

- Present grandparents with a family photo frame and each Christmas give them an updated picture to put in it. There is nothing grandparents love more than pictures to show and enjoy.

Things Grandparents Can Do for their Grandchildren

- Books delight grandchildren. Purchase picture books and read the stories to them on a tape recorder. Use a bell or some other signal when it is time to turn the page. As you read the story you can make comments about the pictures on the pages, naming the child to make it personal. Then, on evenings when the children are tucked into bed, they can fall asleep looking at a story book and hearing Grandma or Grandpa read them the story even though they live many miles away.

- Wrap a gift for each grandchild in a tiny box or mini-stocking and hang it on your tree. All the girls receive the same gift and all the boys the same. Let them take their gifts home from the tree. You may also decide to give another gift for each child besides the treat on the tree.

- Make a memory box by mounting awards, medals, and trophies that show achievements of family members.

- Make or buy new pajamas or nighties for your grandchildren. Include mothers and fathers if you wish.

- If your family is large and your budget small, you might rotate your Christmas giving—boys one year and girls the next.

- On tape, describe to your grandchildren the antics of their parents when they were children. Let them know their parents weren't angels but were lovable children just as they are.

- If you are far away from your grandchildren, adopt a neighbor child and share some of your time. Perhaps you know a child whose grandparents live far away too or are deceased.

- Take a grandchild shopping with you, if he or she is old enough. Children love that special time together.

- Send something in the mail to your little ones—a card or freebie. They love getting their own mail.

- Give some of your treasures and keepsakes to your children and grandchildren who will appreciate them before you leave this earth. Attach a note to the item explaining who it belonged to, who made it, and the sentiment that makes it so special. Evidence of the past lends meaning to the present.

- Save boxes, packages, and so on to create a display in a corner or in a refrigerator box for the children to play store at your home. Run off play money at a copy machine or borrow it from your Monopoly game.

- Set aside a creative corner at your house where the children can make things. Save scraps of odds and ends to paste, draw, cut up, and make pictures with.

- Keep a button jar with buttons of all sorts, sizes, colors.

- Assemble a fabric teaching book from old clothing or from scraps with a variety of colors and textures: fur, velvet, vinyl, wool, silk, corduroy, burlap, cotton, and so forth.

- Sew a quilt for each grandchild (a multiyear project). What a loving and warm memory they all will have. Be sure there will be one for each grandchild as his or her turn comes, because each one will look forward to it.

- Make or purchase a Christmas tree ornament for each of your grandchildren with the child's name on it and the year it was given. When the children leave home for college or marriage, they will have eighteen or so ornaments to put on their first tree away from home.

- Decorate a light switch cover for his/her bedroom.

- Make a set of bean bags with which to play various games.

- Put together a recipe book of your family's favorites over the years and have enough copies printed to give to each child and grandchild.

- Share your favorite crocheting or knitting patterns with your family by writing them out and having them photocopied or printed. Then there will be no need to try to figure out how Grandma made that clever afghan. Pass on your skills and talents if you can see children are interested and have an aptitude for it.

- Make or buy an Advent calendar as suggested in the last chapter. These should be received by December 1st.

- Tape or write a Christmas story of how Grandma and Grandpa used to celebrate Christmas when they were young, particularly if you have a special ethnic background and unique traditions. Also tell how you celebrated Christmas with your children when they were little.

- If you are on a low budget, search out garage sales and pick up used books and toys to give. It won't matter to the children that these gifts aren't brand new; to them, they will be different and fun.

- Listen to your grandchild practice reading. If you live far away, ask the beginning reader to tape-record a book on cassette and mail it to you.

- Help the child start a collection of picture post-cards, souvenir plates or spoons, stamps, coins, salt-and-pepper shakers, thimbles, bells, models, regional dolls, or miniatures. (Just don't start too many types of collections.)

- Buy a child an overnight suitcase and include a small bar of soap, miniature tube of toothpaste, and face towel.

- Set up a small table for bears and dolls by your tree. Invite your grandchild to bring a friend to the Tea Party and have a special time in the land of dreams.

Gifts Of the Heart

Try to **plan into your schedule time for at least one family service activity** that will help reinforce the the true spirit of Christmas, thinking of others instead of just concentrating on getting the preparations over and worrying about what you will give and receive as gifts. If you are lonely, the best cure is to help someone else. Even if you are not lonely— even if you are rushed—compassionate service is still good for the soul. Your acts of goodwill can bless the lives of others for a long time. Make arrangements to visit a hospital, rest home, prison, or other institution. Find someone who will be spending Christmas alone and invite him or her to share Christmas Eve, Christmas Day, or Christmas dinner with you. Think of someone you know who may be a widow or widower, a homebound or handicapped person, a student away from home, or another family who for some reason must have a limited Christmas. As you seek to do good deeds, try to be sensitive to the feelings of the receiver. Sometimes when we reach out in a new way, people don't respond the way we envisioned they would. We may fail despite our good efforts and intentions. Some people "expect" help, but the reward of giving is of such great value that it is worth taking the risk. Sensitize yourself to notice the good things other people are doing.

Helpful-Hand Gifts

- "Adopt" a baby. Contact the Salvation Army or your local church for the name of a needy mother-to-be and prepare a layette, toiletries, and baby equipment to be donated.

- Sponsor a needy child from another country by financing education and welfare through your church or charity.

- Tie up a bundle of firewood with a fancy ribbon and give it to a neighbor or friend who has a fireplace.

- Give a gift of time to share a skill. A mechanic can help teach someone how to care for his or her own car; skilled cooks can share their talent with others. Teach someone to knit, make enchiladas, fix a window, change the oil in a car.

- Give a gift of money through your clergy with instructions to give it anonymously to someone in need.

- Designate a letter night to write to family and friends, missionary, service man or woman.

- Offer to watch a house and take care of plants and pets for a family leaving on a holiday trip.

- Give coupons of service to:
  a) younger brothers and sisters—read stories, play catch, help them learn to rollerskate or ride a bike, drive them somewhere, take their turn at dishes, or let them watch their favorite TV program when it's in conflict with yours.

  b) Mom and Dad—offer to relieve them of Sunday-dinner preparations, take over the cookie baking for the summer, tend younger children, keep parents' shoes polished, sidewalks shoveled, yard trimmed, lawn cut, and so on.

  c) daughters or sons—arrange or give sewing, cooking, or driving lessons, plan an adventure day, go backpacking or fishing.

  d) elderly grandparents—offer help with housework, yard work, grooming, or letter writing; read articles or scriptures; run errands; go shopping; and do other such favors.

- Give a weekly or monthly hour of your time with the receiver choosing how it is to be spent.

- Contact a shelter or group home to see if they need personal items such as shampoo, deodorant, toothbrushes; or gloves and coats; bedding; cooking utensils or food.

Twelve Days of Christmas

The Twelve Days of Christmas in earlier centuries were celebrated after Christmas, ending with January 6th. They were a series of pagan celebrations mixed with Christian saints' birthdays and other events. We are quite removed from these former customs and often base our Twelve Days of Christmas thoughts on the song, "On the first day of Christmas my true love gave to me . . ." Sometimes it is fun to pick up on this theme and perform acts of kindness. Choose someone deserving—mother, father, brother, sister, grandparents, sweetheart, friend, shut-in, minister, handicapped person, neighbor, elderly person, single adult. Give small presents for each of the twelve days before or even after Christmas. If the person lives nearby, it is fun to leave the gift and note each day on the doorstep and run—trying not to be caught. Consider, however, whether this whimsical gesture might be inconvenient for someone who is disabled, elderly, or bedridden; if so, select a different method for delivering your surprises, perhaps via a mutual friend. If the individual lives some distance away, deliver one box or basket on December 13th with twelve packages in it. Wrap each gift and number it 1, 2, 3, and so on. Include a message of love and instructions to open one gift on each of the twelve days. If the person lives far away, you could mail one package each day—fun to receive, but it could be time-consuming for you to stand in those postal lines every day. There are so many varieties of this tradition. One woman gathers garage sale treasures in the summer to give to her friends for the Twelve Days of Christmas fun.

Your gifts could be food items, appropriate for the

diet of the individual, or material gifts like one wreath, two candles, three ornaments, four bright red apples, five candy canes, six Christmas cookies, seven popcorn balls, and so on to a total of twelve. For a young person away from home—someone in the military or a student or missionary, your gift ideas may include a new toothbrush, a roll of postage stamps, stationery, candy, cookies, film for a camera, gum, snapshots of family members, Christmas cups and plates with napkins, dollar bills hidden in walnut shells, love notes from each family member, a very small tabletop artificial tree, a new pair of socks, underwear, fancy nightwear, and favorite snack foods from home (licorice, beef jerky, fruit roll-ups, candy bars, and the like). This project can be lots of fun!

One variation of this custom would be for your family to meet every night for twelve days to prepare surprises for your selected person or family. The excitement mounts during the twelve days as family members think of ideas to include in the box and as the gifts are prepared. On Christmas Eve, deliver all the items. This activity turns thoughts from self to others. Another variation of this theme, a literary one, would be to read a poem, story, or scripture relating to the season with your family group each evening of the twelve days.

Whether you are living alone, are grandparents with an empty nest, or have a home filled with children, seek others to share activities, friendship, and service with. Meet regularly or just occasionally. Remember that goodwill is a commodity that expands to reward both the giver and the receiver.

8th Bite—Memorable Traditions

Traditions are enjoyable activities that are done over and over again. Some are planned and taken on for a specific purpose such as reading from the New Testament and acting out the nativity scene. Some are the result of our cultural heritage, as are the Christmas tree and Santa Claus. Others are spontaneous—for example, the two brothers who started giving a rubber snake back and forth. Each had so much fun trying to disguise the snake and surprise the other one that the joke lasted a decade and was remembered for generations.

Traditions bind our families together. They are comforting. It takes time to build lasting relationships, especially in these times when we are so specialized and transient. Traditions can help us know who we are and build self-esteem. They can give a feeling of continuity, security, and joy in Christmases to come. Traditions passed down from generation to generation will give us roots. Many of our customs involve children, often bringing back our own childhood memories, but traditions can be for adults, too, and the very fact that you observe Christmas is a tradition! Almost everyone on the North American continent decorates a Christmas tree; almost all children hang stockings; most families have a special dinner; many people go to a church service—these are traditions. Making special goodies such as candy, cookies, or fruitcake is an annual tradition. Traditions might be as simple as listening to *The Nutcracker Suite* or attending a holiday concert at the local school. Others can be as complex as putting on a Christmas pageant with extended family or neighbors.

When traditions govern us, however, becoming checklists of things that have to be done, rather than things you want to do, it is time to reevaluate. The most important thing about Christmas traditions is that you have some and that they are yours to use and enjoy, change, or discard—whatever you feel like doing. If you feel like it, break an old tradition that has become bothersome and begin a new one that really appeals to you. **Make a list of the traditions you typically celebrate every year; add the new ones you might like to incorporate, and then prioritize.** With the right traditions you can build positive and strong family ties and make the season special without its becoming so hectic that you are grouchy or depressed. Using an Advent calendar might be a tradition you would like to start for your own young family or for your grandchildren. (See the "6th Bite.") You may intend to continue decorating gingerbread houses. Perhaps you could

73

CHRISTMAS TRADITIONS & IDEAS:		
ITEM	TIME PERIOD	When Trans.
Advent calendar ~ hang it up	Dec 1-25	
Choose a secret family to "pixie"	Dec. 4	
Decorate gingerbread houses	Dec. 22	
Family go carolling to friends & neighbors	Dec. 18-20	

choose a family to "pixie" (to secretly do kind deeds for) this year, bringing great joy to two families—yours and the family you choose. Include these ideas on your list of Christmas traditions and ideas.

In the beginning, Christmas was essentially a day of spiritual observance, without any of the fanfare and color we now have. There were no bells, no carols, no lighted trees, no big banquets. Some claim the added commercialism, frolic, and fun detract from the original intent. We feel you can enjoy these traditions, taking in the glitter, gifts, parties, and food, and still enjoy the peace, goodwill, joy, happiness, and spirituality that are a part of the Christian theology. If we can maintain a pleasant attitude, like a child who doesn't see all the commercialism, if we can organize so the holiday doesn't steal time or money needed for other necessities, if we can gain control of how many extra obligations we take into our lives, we can have that *special* Christmas.

As your life shifts from one stage to another, the emphasis you place on Christmas will change. If your family is young, it is a time of building pleasant memories, showing your love, helping children learn the art of giving and the feeling of compassion. If you are alone or if your children are grown, you can still feel the pleasure of the season, actually having more freedom than parents who are tied to little ones. Use this time of year to show extra charity and do some of the things you have always wanted to do. Loneliness is in the mind, not in living alone. Plan to do things; invite others to your home.

It is a special challenge to keep the gift giving and receiving in its proper perspective and to keep all those materialistic thoughts and desires tucked away where they belong, so that the birth of the Savior can be remembered as the first and foremost purpose of this season. You *can* do it, but it takes planning, preparation, and perseverance.

Plain and Fancy Traditions

• Draw names and for a week become a secret pixie for another immediate family member. Plan special things to do each day without being discovered. The days fill with fun, suspense, surprises, and good deeds, helping to create the true spirit of Christmas.

• Write some gifts to Jesus and hang them on the tree—things individuals need to improve on (such as breaking bad habits and forming good ones). Once a week each family member adds a new gift to concentrate on that coming week.

• Choose a family that needs a lift for the coming Christmas. Someone you know might be having an economic crisis, might have had a recent death in the family, or might be new in your neighborhood—just keep your minds and hearts open and you will find someone who needs a lift. Decide on some personal gifts for them or make up a food basket. Add a game and a few toys and watch the enthusiasm build as the basket fills. Then, on Christmas Eve, put the basket on their doorstep and run! (Sometimes you have to place an anonymous telephone call to alert them that there is a mysterious package on their doorstep.) You can imagine their joy and surprise as they discover the gifts, but nothing can prepare you for the special feeling that comes to your family as you plan and prepare and present a secret act like this—right from your heart—in the *true* spirit of Christmas! If you live in an area where your generous act might be interpreted with suspicion, ask someone who will keep your secret—such as a mutual friend or your minister—to deliver the bundle for you.

- Feature a different country each week; study its traditions; eat something that is part of that nation's cuisine.

- Start a common family hobby such as walking, swimming, cycling, hiking, stamp collecting, photography, music, genealogy, history.

  Enjoy the Santa tradition. Give it as much or as little emphasis as you want. If you do it naturally, without overemphasis, when your children learn the truth, they will accept it as a guise for your love.

- Hold a house-painting party to frost and decorate gingerbread houses.

- Visit Christmas displays in your area—city lights, community trees, window displays, mall decorations.

- Make your child's visit to Santa a pleasant experience by picking a time when you won't be as likely to encounter crowds and long lines. Keep the Santa-and-child snapshots in your Christmas memory album.

- Make cookies with names on them to use as placecards for holiday dinners.

- Start a secular and spiritual Christmas scrapbook of your favorite poems, short stories, and pictures, adding to it each year by watching newspapers and magazines. Include a candid picture of your family each year to show change and growth. This book can become a family treasure.

- Make music a part of your Christmas by including carols for worship and fun songs too. If you aren't musically talented, use the radio or CD player.

- Begin saving Christmas cards, choosing a specific theme: manger scenes, Santa pictures, portraits of the Madonna and Christ child, or winter scenes. Keep your favorites year after year. One woman displays all her nativity cards on the mantle while another family puts all its Santa pictures on cardboard and frames the collection. They make an interesting display, and it's fun to see the change in styles over the years.

- Early in the season, make a wish book. Use a spiral notebook or staple a few pages together. Each person has a page on which to write things he or she would like. It's fun to have a second page for an outrageous list of dream ideas (like a Trans-Am car). Small children could cut pictures from a toy catalog and paste them on their idea list. Keep a record of individual sizes in the back —it could save you from making some exchanges after Christmas.

- Sew up drawstring bags in which to enclose presents so you don't have to wrap all your gifts. They can be filled year after year, and it's a good way of using up some of your leftover fabrics.

- Watch local newspapers for special Christmas plays, musicals, library events, and planetarium shows scheduled for December.

- Hold a weekly Christmas letter night. Make a list of those to whom you wish to write letters. Create or purchase Christmas stationery, and have each family member add a note to each letter written.

- Have a potluck supper with two or three other families or adult couples and then go caroling. Each family could contribute goodies like fruit loaves, canned pickles, jelly, cookies, or popcorn to drop off at the places you chose to carol.

The Tree

The Christmas tree was introduced to America by German settlers in the eighteenth century and has become our national symbol of Christmas. Almost every home and community decorates and lights a tree. In the beginning, real fruit and flowers were the only tree ornaments. Later other foods, such as nuts and cookies and then candles were added. It is believed that because these heavy decorations caused the branches to droop, the German glass blowers began making featherweight glass balls, the beginning of our modern ornaments.

- Go to a forest and choose and cut your own tree (after purchasing a permit, of course). Bring home an extra tree to give someone as a gift. Take along a lunch and hot chocolate. Sing songs, play in the snow, and sleigh ride while on the outing.

- Plan something constructive for young children to do while the adults are checking the lights and putting them on the tree.

- Let the children decorate the tree as high up as they can reach and then have the adults do the upper part.

- Set aside an evening before Christmas to make new and different tree decorations. Watch for ideas within your family's capabilities in craft magazines and books.

- Play carols and sing as you decorate the tree and then have a special meal or treat afterward.

- Some people like to decorate the tree in a new way each year and others prefer the sentimental and traditional decorations they have used in the past.

- Let the children decorate a tree for the playroom and make all their own decorations.

- Place small flags on the Christmas tree to represent the countries where absent family members are living or the countries your ancestors came from.

- Begin collecting small buildings and greenery for a village scene under the tree. Add to it annually. Eventually, you may put up a train to go around the village.

- Decorate your tree with all edibles one year— gingerbread people and candy canes, for example.

- Give or let each child buy his or her own ornament each year to be hung on the family tree. These will become a part of the child's own Christmas treasures when he or she leaves home. They bring memories of Christmases past. This is also a nice traditional gift for grandparents to give to their children and grandchildren.

- Small souvenirs from favorite vacations make interesting tree decorations.

- In some families, the final touch is put on when Dad or Grandpa or some other honored person puts the "angel" on top of the tree. The ornament that tops the tree can become a family heirloom.

- If your space is limited, buy a mini-Christmas tree such as a potted Norfolk pine. After the holiday it makes a nice houseplant.

- Take a picture of the group decorating the tree every year and a picture of the finished product. A collection of these can be added to a memory book.

- Set up a ceramic or wooden nativity scene under the tree.

- If you live in a snowy area, fill small plastic berry baskets with raisins, sunflower seeds, birdseed, popcorn, or dried bread products, mixed with suet or peanut butter to hold it together. This will feed the hungry winter birds and delight the family as they enjoy the different species dining throughout the day.

- Hang candy canes and tiny bags or boxes of treats for children who come to your home as guests.

Christmas Eve

- Have your young family act out the nativity scene while an adult reads from the Scriptures. The children can take parts with costumes made from towels, sheets, and robes, and everyone can sing carols as the story progresses. Take pictures for your Christmas memory book.

- Bake a birthday cake for the Savior. Put one candle on it and light it Christmas Eve or Christmas morning after the gifts are opened to remind everyone whose birthday they are celebrating.

- Have a traditional Christmas Eve supper. This could be early so the young children can participate, or a late dinner, even after midnight service, for adults only. Serve something special that everyone enjoys but that is different from what you generally eat. It could be something like boiled shrimp or oyster stew. It might also be an ethnic dish that has been passed down in your family through the generations, or it could be something very simple like brown bread and milk such as the Jews would have eaten 2,000 years ago.

- Include a talent show in your Christmas Eve program, with each of the family members participating in story, poem, song, or musical instrument performances. Invite grandparents and take lots of pictures.

- Some families like to have each child open one gift on Christmas Eve, often new pajamas or nighties to wear that night for sweet dreams and pretty pictures tomorrow.

- Video tape your Christmas Eve activities for future enjoyment or to send to absent family members.

- Grandparents often enjoy visiting on Christmas Eve and staying overnight so they don't miss any of the special early-morning activity and excitement with the young children.

- Hanging the stockings is always an important activity. Some hang them by the fireplace, others individually on certain chairs or the sofa. In other homes the stockings are brought out after the children are in bed, and they magically appear, all filled, on Christmas morning.

- Some families have matching stockings for each family member with the individual's names on them. Other families have very different stockings for each member that they readily identify from one year to the next.

- One family serves a big rice pudding on Christmas Eve with one almond in it. Whoever gets the almond wins a special gift or treat to share with the rest of the family (a new game to play, a puzzle, or a box of candy).

- After the children get into their nightwear, turn the tree lights on and the rest of the lights off, and let everyone lie on the carpet around the tree and sing a couple of quiet songs. Have one of the adults tell a special Christmas story that will calm down the little ones before bedtime. This is more personal than "watching another TV special."

- In some homes, a friend is invited to dress up as Santa and visit on Christmas Eve. Each individual, even each adult, sits on Santa's lap, tells him the good things done in the past year, and lists the goals set for the coming new year (better than just asking for things!).

- While some choose to make Christmas Eve their spiritual observance, others read special poems or stories like *The Night Before Christmas,* or *How the Grinch Stole Christmas* by Dr. Seuss. Begin a library of these special Christmas story books; add a new one every year.

- Include a small special gift in the toe of the Christmas stocking—something unusual that will be prized and treasured and anticipated each year. In some homes, this small gift is saved until last when everyone opens their presents together.

- Leave Santa a snack and a thank-you note.

- Make a Yule Log—a piece of firewood decorated with ribbon and pinecones—to burn on Christmas Eve. In Europe the Yule Log is hidden in the woods, and finding it brings one good fortune.

- Many families have traditional stocking stuffers—apples, oranges, popcorn balls, nuts, candies, new toothbrushes, small boxes of favorite cereal for Christmas morning with a can of juice and a straw. Other well-received items are: shoelaces (plain or fancy), Band-aids, cosmetics, crayons, novelty calendars, pencils, erasers, lip balm sticks, balloons, uniquely shaped pens and soaps, whistles (if you dare), magnets, flashlights, batteries, padlocks and keys, mini-cars, jump ropes, jacks, marbles, washable magic markers, bubbles, play money, gift certificates for ice cream and hamburgers, and theater tickets.

- Sleep under the Christmas tree, together as a family.

Christmas Day

- Awaken your family by getting up ahead of them (if this is possible) and caroling from room to room. Have each family member join in the parade as the group gets closer to the lighted tree and the cozy fire burning in the fireplace.

- Barricade the door with newspapers taped over the doorway until the entire family is up on

Christmas morning when everyone can go in together.

- Some families have everyone get up and dress and eat breakfast before they open gifts. Others eat a snack, open gifts, and then fix a big sausage-and-waffle breakfast.

- Put breakfast into your children's stockings—rolls and sliced oranges, wrapped and ready.

- If you have a lot of family members in your city, you might try a progressive breakfast where everyone meets at one home for juice and to look at that family's gifts and wish them a Merry Christmas. Then the entire group moves to the next home for bacon and eggs, then on for sweet rolls and a hot drink. Single adults could easily adopt this idea and have a progressive breakfast with their friends.

- Stretch out the fun by letting everyone open one gift at a time before anyone else gets a second. Appoint one person to be Santa and deliver the gifts to one individual at a time.

- Assign the children fun duties Christmas morning —one is in charge of delivering packages, another is the ribbon-and-bow chairman, another is the paper disposer, another is the fire builder (not necessarily the fire *lighter*), another is the tree lighter, and so forth. Older children could be responsible for helping younger ones to open and record their gifts.

- Invite someone who must spend Christmas alone to share your Christmas Day and dinner. Remember the single, lonely, elderly, and handicapped.

- It is often traditional to phone distant family and friends on this day. Watch out! Sentimentality can cost you more than you can afford on phone calls. Remember, it is Ma Bell who pays for the commercials that tell us a "phone call is the next best thing to being there!" If you must make long-distance calls, write yourself a "script" and hold to it to keep your call to a reasonable length. You might also consider sending a tape-recorded message by mail instead of making a phone call.

- In one home it is a tradition to start a new jigsaw puzzle on Christmas Day. The family has a wooden frame in which to put the pieces so the puzzle can be moved off the dining table when it is time for dinner.

- Break a piñata on Christmas night—save some things to do later in the day so that all of Christmas isn't over by 7:00 A.M.

9th Bite—It's Over! Now What?

For most children, the school vacation isn't over on Christmas Day. They still have a week at home. Many adults arrange to have time off from work during the interim until New Year's Day. **Anticipate a letdown at this time and save some things to do.** In some families it is a time for bargain shopping; for others it means going skiing. By now many homes need some housecleaning, at least taking down the decorations. Perhaps you can offer an incentive like going to the movies to enlist children's help in getting the decorations carefully placed in labeled boxes. The Nelson family saves one little gift for each person, to be opened after all the decorations are put away.

After-Christmas Traditions

- An old European custom, Boxing Day, was started by employers giving pottery boxes to their paid servants with money rewards inside. For those who rendered a regular service to many, each employer dropped a coin in the worker's box. The day after Christmas (the servants had to work on Christmas Day), the servants had a day off, and they also broke open their clay boxes. The British and Canadians still celebrate Boxing Day as a play-holiday, because Christmas Day is more of a religious observance. In the United States, many of us go shopping—to exchange things, to take advantage of good sales, to spend our Christmas money. We could call it a Boxing Day of sorts—a day to bring home more things that will eventually be stored in boxes.

• Have a "break-the-gingerbread-house party" the day after Christmas. Each child invites a friend to come and bring one of his or her favorite presents. They show and tell and then break the gingerbread house and eat it!

• If you have any leftover Christmas cards and don't want to send the same ones to your friends next year, have a brunch with your friends and swap leftover cards.

• Don't be tempted to chop the Christmas tree up into small pieces to burn later. This causes a flammable coating to form in your chimney! Rather, put the tree outside, leaving the popcorn and cranberry garlands on it for the birds to enjoy.

• Save some of the used wrapping paper to line drawers and linen-closet shelves. This gives children something to do during holiday vacation—straightening their drawers.

• When the tree is dismantled (Knuts day), redecorate it with bread and suet pieces and put it in the yard for the birds.

  In an effort to recycle, some communities advertise a drop-off site to gather trees which they grind up and offer back to the community as free mulch in the Spring.

Take Time for Thank-You's

Take time to help your family write thank-you notes. It is a good discipline, and if the lesson is learned well, your rewards will come when you are a grandparent and your children help their children show appreciation. We often hear the lament, "I worked so hard on that gift; a little thank-you would make me feel it was worth the effort." Take the time to express those golden words. If you are fortunate enough to be around those who gave you and your family gifts, encourage children to express verbal appreciation. Receiving gifts graciously is a skill that can be learned. Thank-you's are usually voiced when gifts are opened, but make it a point to give a second thoughtful expression sometime later. "That doily looks beautiful on our dining table. I know how much time you spent making it and I treasure your gift." Even if the gift was not what you wanted, appreciation can be expressed for the effort and kind thought. Every gift has something good about it.

75

Was Christmas the Way I Wanted It?

Take a few minutes to reflect on the past Christmas season and answer some questions. Was Christmas all you had hoped? What would you have done differently? Can you make it better next year? Do you need to cut down? Are there some long-term projects you would like to start early (like knitted afghans, crocheted stars, ceramics, wood projects)? Write down your evaluation and suggestions and plans. This sounds so easy, but most people won't take the time to do it even though it is a fundamen-

76

tal principle of successful time management. Keep the notes in your journal or planning notebook or in the back of your address book, or scribble them in the margins of this book. Give it thirty minutes and you will be well on your way to a pleasant Christmas next year, even if you don't look at your notes again until Thanksgiving. You won't hit the target goal unless you have plans. Record your ideas for next year and reflect on the successes of the past year. So many things happen between one Christmas and the next, you could lose some good ideas.

Look over the following evaluation questions to stimulate your planning.

1. What things would I have liked to do for the past Christmas but time ran out on me? (List them.) _____

2. Which of these things could I plan now to do earlier in the next year so I won't run out of time again? _____

3. How many people did we give to this year? _____   _____
              (major gift)   (token gift)

(Record names and gifts if you wish on the inside back cover of the book.)

4. How much did I spend this year? $ _____
   Did I go over my budget? _____
   If I did overspend, could I cut down next year?
   _____ Is opening a Christmas savings
   (yes/no)
   account the answer? _____
                 (yes/no)

5. Do I still have any promised Christmas gifts to

finish? _____ Could I have given a substitute
     (yes/no)
gift rather than committing my January and February time to a Christmas past? _____
                          (yes/no)

6. Did we overindulge the children? _____
                           (yes/no)
Shall we cut back next year? _____
                         (yes/no)
Can we coordinate their gifts with others? Shall we put away some of the toys and games for a few months and bring them out when something new will be appreciated? _____
                         (yes/no)

7. Will my gift list change before next year—will there be any new in-laws, new babies, new neighbors, or new friends to add? (List them.)

_____

8. (If you draw names in your family.) Is there any reason why we couldn't draw names early in the year instead of waiting until November? _____
     (yes/no)

(Perhaps you could even put everyone that you draw names with on a rotation list and give copies to those participating, which will let you know whose names you will draw this year, and for the next few years as well.)

9. Did I do enough baking or too much? _____
How much did I bake or buy? _____
_____

10. What baked items and snacks did my family really enjoy most? _____

Did I gain weight? How can I protect myself from over-indulging?

11. What decorations and tree ornaments would I like to add or change for next year? _____
   _____

12. Were my cards and family letters written and mailed on time? _____ What will be my tar-
   (yes/no)
   get date next year? _____ How many did I send? _____ cards _____ letters

13. Were my gifts mailed before deadlines? _____
   (yes/no)
   Did they arrive before Christmas? _____
   (yes/no)
   How early do I need to mail them next year? _____

14. Did we enjoy the last week before Christmas because we were prepared and relaxed? _____
   (yes/no)

15. What did we do to keep the kids busy? _____

16. What did we do Christmas Eve? _____

17. What did we do Christmas Day? _____
   Were we relaxed or were we too ex-
   hausted? _____

18. Did we do something special this year as a ser-
   vice project to make Christmas meaningful to someone outside our family? _____
   (yes/no)

   (Describe it.) _____

19. What did we do this year to make Christmas really meaningful *with* our family? _____
   _____

20. Was the celebration of the birth of the Savior an important part of our Christmas festivities? _____
      (yes/no)

21. What traditions would I like to add or change for next year? _____
_____

22. What projects would I like to do next year? (Check the time you would like to start them. We are all optimistic at this time of year about getting a head start on next Christmas.)

Project	Now	Spring	Summer	Fall
_____	___	____	____	____
_____	___	____	____	____
_____	___	____	____	____
_____	___	____	____	____

Last Bite—Recipes, from Us to You

Now that you've gotten this far, we just want to share a few quick and easy recipes—our families' Christmas favorites—with you.

BONNIE'S RYE BREAD

2 3/4 cups very warm
   tap water
1/4 cup oil or margarine
1/4 cup molasses
1/4 cup of brown sugar
1 1/2 tablespoons yeast

2 1/2 cups rye flour
1 1/2 tablespoons salt
5 cups white flour
1 tablespoon whole
   caraway seeds
   (optional)

Put very warm tap water, oil, molasses, and sugar into large bowl. Stir to dissolve sugar. Add yeast; let set until yeast is working. Add rye flour and salt, and stir vigorously. Add caraway seeds. Add white flour gradually until a workable dough is attained. Let rest 10 minutes. Knead 10 minutes. Let rise until double in bulk; punch down and divide into two parts. Let rest for 10 minutes. Make into two round loaves; set in two 9-inch round cake pans or pie tins and let rise until double in bulk. Slash the top with a sharp knife or razor blade. Bake at 375 degrees for 45 minutes. Remove from oven, brush with glaze made with 1/2 cup water and approximately 1 1/2 teaspoons cornstarch, brought to a boil. This gives the loaf a pretty shine. (The texture of this bread improves if dough is allowed to rise a second time before being made into loaves.)

JACKIE'S CARAMEL CORN

Combine 1 1/3 cups white sugar, 1/2 cup margarine, and 1/2 cup white corn syrup. Boil 6 minutes. Remove from heat and stir in 1 teaspoon vanilla. Pour over mixture of 3 quarts popcorn, 1 1/2 cups whole or half pecans, and 2/3 cup toasted and slivered almonds. Pour onto cookie sheet and break apart when dry, *or* form into balls before it cools. Makes 3 quarts of caramel corn or 12–18 popcorn balls.

CLAUDIA'S BANANA SLUSH

Heat and dissolve 4 cups white sugar and 6 cups water. Combine in blender with 2 1/2 cups orange juice, 1/2 cup lemon juice, 4 cups pineapple juice, and 5 mashed bananas. Color if desired by adding powdered Kool-Aid. Put in quart containers and store in freezer. When ready to use, chop up lightly. Fill glasses half-full of frozen mixture and add ginger ale or 7-up. Makes about one gallon. Great! Easy. Wonderful to have on hand for unexpected company.

MONSTER COOKIES

3 eggs
1 cup packed brown
  sugar
1 cup white sugar
1 teaspoon vanilla
1 teaspoon corn syrup
2 teaspoons baking
  soda

1 stick margarine
  (1/2 cup)
1 1/2 cups peanut butter
4 1/2 cups quick oatmeal
2/3 cup chocolate chips
1/4 pound M&M plain
  chocolate candies

Beat eggs. Cream with margarine and sugar. Add remaining ingredients. Mix. Place on ungreased cookie sheet using ice cream scoop, for giant cookies. Bake at 350 degrees for 12–15 minutes. (These cookies can also be made regular size; just use teaspoonsful and bake for 10–12 minutes.)

GRANDMA COOPER'S CRANBERRY JELLY

To 4 cups fresh or frozen berries, add 3 cups water and cook until soft. Put through strainer while hot. Put back on stove and measure 3/4 cup sugar to each cup of juice. Heat juice until it boils; add sugar and stir until sugar is dissolved. Boil rapidly for 5 minutes. Pour into jars and seal with wax. Makes about 6 half-pints of jelly.

GRANDMA DAISY'S GERMAN COOKIES

Great Do-ahead cookies; the longer they stand, the better they taste.
Beat together:
2 cups soft brown sugar
2 eggs
1 cup butter or margarine
Mix:
1 teaspoon baking soda
1 teaspoon baking powder
4 tablespoons sour milk*
Add:
1/2 teaspoon each of cloves, nutmeg and
   cinnamon
1 1/2 cups raisins
2 cups chopped nuts
3/4 cups white flour (enough to make stiff dough)

Let dough stand over night to chill. No need to grease cookie sheet. Use one tablespoon dough for each cookie, flatten dough with fork. Bake 375 degrees for 8–10 minutes or until brown. When cool, put in crock or covered container; they will stay soft. Cookies are better the longer they stand. Three times this recipe makes one gallon crockful.

BEV'S CHERRY LOAF

Cream 1/2 cup butter until fluffy. Add 5/8 cup sugar and beat till creamy. Add 2 well-beaten eggs. Mix in

---

* To make fresh milk sour, put a little lemon juice or vinegar into the sweet milk and let stand a few minutes

2 tablespoons milk, 1/2 teaspoon lemon extract, 1/2 teaspoon almond extract, and 1/2 teaspoon vanilla extract. Sift 1 1/4 cups flour, 1 teaspoon baking powder, and 1/4 teaspoon salt and add to mixture. Add 1/4 cup slivered almonds, 3/4 cup glacé or well-drained maraschino cherries, halved. Add 2 teaspoons lemon juice. Pour into a greased loaf pan and bake for 60 minutes at 325 degrees.

BARBARA'S CHEESE BALL

8-ounce package cream cheese

8-ounce package sharp cheddar cheese

Walnuts, chopped

2-ounce package blue cheese

1 tablespoon Worcestershire sauce

Soften all cheeses to room temperature. Mash cheddar cheese with a fork until well blended. Add cream cheese and blue cheese. Blend in Worcestershire sauce. Add a few chopped walnuts. Put in cheese dish. Sprinkle remaining nuts on top. Store in refrigerator if it is to be used within a week; otherwise freeze.

BEV'S HOT SPICED CIDER

Heat 6 quarts of apple juice. Tie into a little square of cheesecloth bag 4 sticks cinnamon, 12 whole cloves, 1 teaspoon whole alspice. Drop bag into hot juice and add 1/2 cup brown sugar. Boil 5 minutes, stirring frequently. Remove bag of spices. Add 4 cups orange juice, 3/4 cup lemon juice, and 1 cup cranberry juice. Heat to just below boil and serve hot with thin slice of orange floating on top. (You can leave the spice bag in longer if you want a slightly stronger flavor.)

GRANDMA O'NEIL'S STEAM PUDDING SAUCE

Cook until clear 1 scant tablespoon cornstarch, 1 cup brown sugar, 1 cup water, and 1 tablespoon white vinegar. Add 1 teaspoon vanilla and heaping tablespoon of butter. Stir in and serve hot over Christmas steamed pudding.

ANN'S DUTCH SOUP

Cover a large soup bone and 1 pound stewing beef with water. Bring to a boil, then cover and simmer all day and the next morning. Take out all bones and meat and add salt and pepper and a few shakes each of clove, nutmeg, Worcestershire sauce, and paprika. Also add 6 or 7 beef bouillon cubes, 2 stalks of finely chopped celery including all celery leaves and tops, 5 or 6 chopped carrots, one whole onion, and 1/4 package vermicelli broken up (cauliflower, string beans, peas, or corn can be added if you have any left over). Add 2 tablespoons dry parsley and one package of dry spring-vegetable soup mix. Chop up meat and add. Boil and simmer at least one hour. About 45 minutes before serving, add 1 pound lean hamburger made into tiny meatballs. Continue simmering. (This is a delicious European-style thick soup).

CHRISTMAS JELL-O SALAD

1/2 cup red hots
1/2 cup boiling water
2 apples, shredded

3-ounce package cherry
  Jell-O
1 cup boiling water
1/2 cup nuts

Set red hots in bowl with 1/2 cup boiling water for about 15 minutes to dissolve the candies. Dissolve the cherry gelatin in 1 cup boiling water. Mix candy water and dissolved gelatin, then add shredded apples and chopped nuts if desired. A douple recipe fills a 9-by-13 inch pan.

PAM'S EASY PEANUT BRITTLE

1 cup corn syrup
1 tablespoon butter
1 cup sugar
1 teaspoon soda

3/4 teaspoon salt
1 12-ounce package
  raw peanuts

Mix syrup, butter, sugar, and salt over heat until sugar melts. Add 12-ounce package raw peanuts. Cook until peanuts are light brown. Add 1 teaspoon soda. Spread thinly over greased cookie sheet. Cool.

CRACKER JACKS

Mix 1 cube margarine (1/2 cup), 1 cup corn syrup, and 1 cup brown sugar and boil for five minutes. Remove from heat and add 1 teaspoon vanilla, 1/2 teaspoon soda. Pour over 12–14 cups popcorn. Bake at 250 degrees for 30 minutes, stirring every 5 minutes.

You can order extra copies of this book and copies of Bonnie McCullough's previous books through your local bookstore, or directly from St. Martin's Press, 175 Fifth Avenue, New York, N.Y. 10010.

ORDER FORM

Please send:

0-312-92940-4 _____ copies of *76 Ways To Get Organized For Christmas* at $3.99

0-312-80747-3 _____ copies of *Totally Organized* at $11.95

0-312-30147-2 _____ copies of *401 Ways to Get Your Kids to Work at Home* at $8.95

0-312-08708-X _____ copies of *Bonnie's Household Budget Book* (revised, available 1/93) at $8.95

0-312-08795-0 _____ copies of *Bonnie's Household Organizer* at $6.95

Enclose postage and handling charges of $2.00 for the first book and 75¢ for each additional book. Payable in U.S. funds. Send check or money order to St. Martin's Press, 175 Fifth Avenue, New York, N.Y. 10010

Total amount enclosed: _____

Name _____

Address _____

City _____ State _____ Zip _____

Now, at last . . . a day-planner designed especially for the homemaker!

The *Homemaker's Executive Day-planner* is a professional organization and planning system designed to keep track of all of the many-faceted activities that a home executive is responsible for. Its 9- by 6-inch looseleaf format allows for flexibility to suit the personal needs of the busy mother, full-time or part-time homemaker, business person, college student, or active grandparent. Your choice of various hole-punch styles. Burgundy or brown binder. Packet includes tabbed dividers, daily pages and special planning sections for holidays, birthdays, goals, shopping, money, etc.

For further information, write to *Homemaker's Executive Day-planner*, P.O. Box 594, Kaysville, Utah 84037, or call 1-(800)-544-0699.

Name _____

Address _____

City _____ State _____ Zip _____

Phone _____ - _____
      area

Index

COOKING? DIETING?
HERE'S HELP!

NONFICTION PERENNIALS
FROM ST. MARTIN'S PAPERBACKS

25 THINGS YOU CAN DO TO BEAT THE RECESSION OF THE 1990s
Alan Weintraub and Pamela Weintraub
_____ 92646-4 $3.95 U.S./$4.95 Can.

THE PEOPLE'S PHARMACY
Joe Graedon
_____ 91762-7 $5.95 U.S.   _____ 91763-5 $6.95 Can.

HOW TO STAY LOVERS WHILE RAISING YOUR CHILDREN
Anne Mayer
_____ 92715-0 $4.99 U.S./$5.99 Can.

76 WAYS TO GET ORGANIZED FOR CHRISTMAS
Bonnie McCullough & Bev Cooper
_____ 91253-6 $2.95 U.S.   _____ 91254-4 $3.95 Can.

YOU CAN SAVE THE ANIMALS: 50 Things to Do Right Now
Dr. Michael W. Fox and Pamela Weintraub
_____ 92521-2 $3.95 U.S./$4.95 Can.

CHILD CARE BOOKS YOU CAN COUNT ON—

from ST. MARTIN'S PAPERBACKS

BEYOND JENNIFER AND JASON
Linda Rosenkrantz and Pamela Redmond Satran
Newly updated, this landmark book is truly the *only* guide you'll need to naming your baby!
_____ 92331-7 $4.95 U.S./$5.95 Can.

GOOD BEHAVIOR
Stephen W. Garber, Ph.D., Marianne Daniels Garber, and Robyn Freedman Spizman
This comprehensive, bestselling guide lists answers to over a thousand of the most challenging childhood problems.
_____ 92134-9 $5.95 U.S./$6.95 Can.

THE SELF-CALMED BABY
William A.H. Sammons, M.D.
Strung-out babies *can* calm themselves—and this one-of-a-kind guide shows you how to help them do it!
_____ 92468-2 $4.50 U.S./$5.50 Can.

EXPERT CHILD-CARE ADVICE AND HELP—

from St. Martin's Paperbacks

—◦◦◦◦—

FAMILY RULES
Kenneth Kaye, Ph.D.
Here's how to custom-design a straightforward set of rules
on discipline that will fit *your* family.
_____ 92369-4 $4.95 U.S./$5.95 Can.

THE FIRST FIVE YEARS
Virginia E. Pomeranz, M.D., with Dodi Schultz
The classic guide to baby and child care, including answers
to the 33 most-asked questions.
_____ 90921-7 $3.99 U.S./$4.99 Can.

BABY SIGNALS
**Diane Lynch-Fraser, Ed.D., and Ellenmorris Tiegerman,
Ph.D.**
There are four distinct styles which infants communicate
with—and this book tells you what they are and how to
respond.
_____ 92456-9 $3.99 U.S./$4.99 Can.